Once Upon A Time In Glasgow's Oatlands

Danny Gill

Copyright © 2018 Danny Gill

All rights reserved, including the right to reproduce this book, or portions thereof in any form. No part of this text may be reproduced, transmitted, downloaded, decompiled, reverse engineered, or stored, in any form or introduced into any information storage and retrieval system, in any form or by any means, whether electronic or mechanical without the express written permission of the author.

The views expressed in this work are solely those of the author and do not necessarily reflect the views of the publisher, and the publisher hereby disclaims any responsibility for them.

Front cover photo: This is the red bricked Steamie that once stood in Fauldhouse Street in Oatlands.

ISBN: 978-0-244-66648-4

PublishNation
www.publishnation.co.uk

Other books by Danny Gill which can be bought from Lulu.com and Amazon as either a paperback or a Kindle ebook.

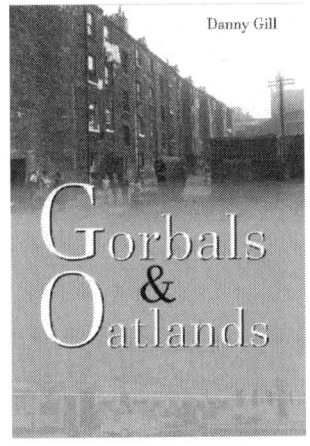

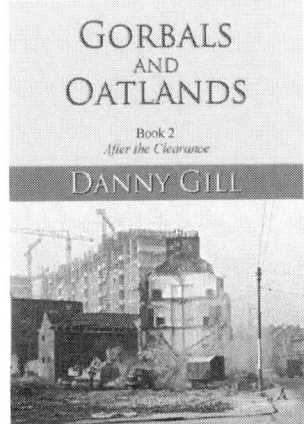

All proceeds from this book will be shared equally between:-

The upkeep of the Southern Necropolis Graveyard on Caledonia Road in the Gorbals area of Glasgow; and

The Benny Lynch statue campaign.

My sincerest thanks to everyone who purchases this book.

Danny Gill

Foreword

I have tried to take us on a walk through the old streets of Oatlands to the time when the old tenements were still standing. I have based the area of Oatlands from Braehead street to Queensferry street/Rosyth street. This is the area that I classed as Oatlands everything else after Braehead street to Crown street is the Hutchesontown district of the Gorbals in my view. [some may disagree which is OK by me as we all hold different views]

That tenement area of Oatlands was such a brilliant place to grow up in back in the 1950's/60's but sadly with the collapse of the back of my tenement in Decemeber 1960 my family had to leave the soo side behind us and move to one of the new housing schemes which I never really settled in. I always kept going back there as this is where I felt that I belonged, that close knit community spirit that we all enjoyed, the company of your wee pals out playing all kinds of games under the watchful eyes of our elders who would be doing their bit of "windae hingin" and catching up on the local news.

People back then seemed to have more time for everyone, and would go out of their way to help each and other, and it is this abiding memory that I have tried to capture when I take us all on a walk through the old streets that we used to know. With my mentioning the different shop names and people's names as we take a walk through the streets I hope to bring back plenty of memory's to you also my friends. Overall I believe that Glasgow council planners have carried out a good job with the regeneration of Oatlands but the Oatlands area that I grew up in will always hold a special place in my heart, because the old tenements with all their faults was such a wonderful place to live in.

I also know that in a hundred years time from now that era of Oatlands that we all shared and lived in will still be getting talked about, we had so many shops to choose from, so many street games to play, Shawfield stadium for Clyde FC and the greyhounds on our doorstep and our very own Richmond park, well who could have asked for anymore. !!

So I hope you enjoy the trip back to Oatlands, as it was, "Once upon a time."

Acknowledgements

First of all I would like to offer my thanks to all the people who helped me so much with giving me the names of shops and their positions, I have tried my best to get them in the correct order but remember that over the years shops changed not only their names but their positions too, so please forgive me if I have got any wrong as we are going back 50 and 60 years ago so if I do make any mistakes I offer my apologies in advance.

Also thanks to everyone for the help they gave me in telling me what closes people stayed up, there are so many of you that I have to thank, there are so many to name that it would take me forever so I would like to say a big thank you again , you know who you all are and many thanks friends.

Once again I would like to give thanks/credits for all my photos/info to my good friend Norrie McNamee [who has helped me with photos for my books over the years, thanks Norrie,] James Currie, Raymond Depardon, Duncan Macallum, Urban Glasgow website, Evening Times and my friend Peter Mortimer for his advice and help.

I would also like to thank David and Gwen at PublishNation for all their help in getting my book published.

Also my thanks to James "Jamie" McKenzie who planted the seed into my brain about doing a book about Oatlands about four years ago when he said "I don't know how to go about writing a book about Oatlands but if I did then I would certainly do it" and Linda Stephenson who prompted me last year to do it. So here you are Linda and Jamie. !!

Last but not least a big thanks to everyone who takes the time to read my book, it actually has been a labour of love for me to write it.

This book is dedicated to everyone who has ever lived in that area of south Glasgow that we call Oatlands.

Question: Do you know anyone famous fae Oatlands?

Answer: Aye, all oor Ma's and Da's.

CHAPTER 1

Poems

The Pawn Shop.

In the Tenements of Old, with our people living on the edge.
The Pawn Shop was oor saviour, with your articles to pledge.

Nobody liked to be caught going in, it did take a bit of nerve.
If you saw a neighbour, then you gave them the body swerve.

Pawn shops wur a plenty in Glasgow, ye cood pawn anything.
Wrist watches to wedding dresses even your engagement ring.

Every Monday mornin my Da's suit wiz pledged, so it seemed.
But on a Friday night, Ma went back there to get it Redeemed.

Cash wiz tight and oor Mothers would give each other a haun.
Although as a last resort they really thanked God fur the Pawn.

My generation remember the Pawn while some say it's a fable.
But if it wizzny fur "Uncle" there'd be nae food upon the table

So now my poem is over hopefully a smile comes to your face.
Cos to survive in them days gaun to the Pawn was no disgrace.

Queen o the Steamie.

She wiz Queen of the Steamie, her name = Agnes McSweeney.
Filled her pram wae washin, shirt's, skirt's and a dirty old peeny

Lived wae her man three stairs up, in a Single End in oor street
Always first in finishing her washin Agnes was never once beat.

Doing her washing, she shared the gossip above the racket n din
Hear the scandal aboot big Ella, she got caught out living in Sin.

And what aboot free and easy Isa, her new baby it's called Davy
Yet her man's been gone for two years, wae the Merchant Navy

She went back to her house, resting her feet while drinking Tea
C'os she left the Steamie early, hoping they don't talk aboot me

The Steamie had another function, giving oor Agnes great hope
For a tanner you got a hot bath with a towel and Carbolic Soap

Lifes changed today as kitchens hiv washin machins so dreamy
A long time noo since oor Agnes, wiz the Queen o the Steamie.

The Single End.

We aw knew someone who lived there, neighbour or a friend.
That wee hoose in the middle of the landing, wiz a single end.

T'was a small dwelling by Health n Saftey that we know today.
My Granny, Granda and dug lived in wan, jist two closes away.

This wee single end wiz yir living room n kitchen more or less
Then there wiz this Alcove with a curtain, it was yer bed recess

Wee lobby wae a coal bunker, door shut to keep oot all the dust.
2 chairs and a Table in the middle to eat on, always was a must

Aye the single end was so rare n cosy, the coal fire so appealing
Dryin yir wet clothes on the Pulley above hingin fae the ceiling

I remember sat there wae my wee Granny listenin to her singin
She made us a cuppa tea, and we done a bit of Windae Hinging

The single ends hiv all gone, but in my mind they still do stand
When growing up in the tenements, for us aw was oh so Grand.

The Whistling Kettle.

Ma's Kitchen had many things, tins of Vim to bottles of Dettol.
But I know her pride and joy was that auld tin Whistling Kettle.

She used it fur oh so many Chore's, carrying oot her Daily Toil.
The gas always kept on a peep so it wouldn't take long tae boil.

When the kettle whistled alerting oor Ma's to their job in hand.
Like fillin up the hot watter bottle makin the bed warm n grand

Her turn came round to wash the stair's she done it withoot fail.
The Whistlin kettle wae its boiling watter filed up oor Ma's pail

As weans all hating that night, for that Auld Tin Bath of metal.
Waiting oor turn until Ma said, right you're next my wee petal.

Just a few jobs that the whistling kettle done Im sure you agree.
But most important job was for Granny, making us a pot of Tea

Today we have kitchen's, with Cordless Kettle's made of Plastic
Who recalls the whistlin kettle when tenement life wiz fantastic.

The Pictures.

Before TV + Video's and the Internet, took all our live's over.
Gaun to the pictures was as good as finding a four leaf clover.

The Usherette wid be shining her Torch, for us tae find a seat.
' Cos if she diddny, it was so dark, you might trip over yer feet.

The Movies could show James Cagney or the lovely Doris Day.
At Interval time, the lassie came round with the ice-cream tray.

The back row was for the Winchers, aw cuddling and a kissing.
Never seeming to mind the film that both of them wur missing.

And Saturday Matinee's had films for us weans, so dead funny.
Oor Ma's hid given us aw the entrance fee with pocket money.

Then TV took over, no longer we went to the Balcony or Stalls.
Because oor local picture hoose's got turned intae Bingo Halls.

Nowadays I'm an O.A.P. and my diary hasn't got many fixtures.
I remember with great pleasure my times gaun tae the Pictures.

Wedding Scramble.

I think of an event years ago I explain it without any preamble.
As one and all we aw got ready, for that wedding day scramble.

Bride and Groom jist newly married, looked so happy n sweet.
Covered in confetti, they went intae the Wedding car back seat

Then as the car did edge away, the car windae it wound down.
As a handful of coin's got chucked out, landing on the ground.

All Hell broke loose as the coins got thrown, Oh whit a scatter.
Men, Women and weans aw dived in, sure age it diddny matter.

Pushing and shuvin and elbows used, trying fur a penny or two.
Somebody got a broken finger and some poor wean lost a shoe.

The lucky wans who got a Penny, went to spend it in the Shop.
Unlucky wans looked a mess, as the one shoe wean did a Hop.

Getting married and having a family is all part of life's gamble.
Not a patch as diving in heid first, at the wedding day scramble.

Spinnin the Bottle.

Today we have Hi Fi systems to hear oor music at full throttle.
The tenements had few record players, we wid spin the bottle.

Pubs all closed at 10 o'clock pm but we were never at a loose.
Cos we wid buy a kerry oot and have a party in sumdys hoose.

The drink poured and glasses filled so to quench aw oor thirst.
Then we would spin the bottle, to see who wid be singing first.

Bottle stopped spinnin, its neck pointing at first to sing a song.
Giving it Laldy, the singer sang oot in a voice shaky but strong.

Everybody took their turn to sing, fast or dead smoochy slow.
Even if the Guy knocked the ceiling, fae his hoose doon below.

We wur enjoying oorselves, but the kerry-oot diddny last long.
Oor appointed MC shouting oot, "c'mon wan singer wan song".

Aye we all knew how to Party, in those Tenement's of the past
As we dutifully spun the bottle, belting song's oot at full blast.

Windae Hingin.

Remember the Tenement's of years ago, in my memory I dredge.
I kin see my Ma and my Granny,all leanin on their windae ledge.

We called it windae hingin, speakin to your neighbours next door.
With a pillow or cushion under yer elbow's, as they cood get sore.

Chattin to yer pals either side, ye'd hear aw aboot peoples Capers.
The news got passed by word of mouth, who needed newspapers.

Aye lookin from yer street windae when doinn yer windae hingin.
Yer kitchen windae saw the back court, the middens were mingin.

Watchin the drunks coming oot of the pub,they held us in a trance.
With a fish supper stuck in their pockets, singing n trying to dance.

Then a wummin from across the street, started makin a big racket.
Aw naw that's my man I hope he hizzny spent aw his wage packet.

Then tenements got demolished replaced wae buildings so dreamy.
And windae hingin's a thing o the past jist like gaun to the steamie.

The Midgie Raker.

In the days of Gasgow auld when aw the Tenements did abound.
It was in the back courts, that the Midgie Raker was to be found.

Now Midgie Rakin wiz an Art, searching for treasures all hidden.
Wearing short troosers n wellies diving head first into the midden.

But Tony Wilson wae his younger brother they sure were the best.
Raking Midgies form early mornin till late at night with such zest.

Searching in aw the Middens, wiz like gaun through Gold coffers.
When a luxy was found the shout went up "ah'm baggin Haufers".

They raked aw day and with their loot they were king of the castle.
Keeping an eye oot fur the polis who sometimes gave them hassle.

Swappin aw their loot for sweeties, with the other weans in barter.
No flies on the the Midgie Raker's, they diddny come any smarter.

Noo their Midgie rakin days are over they never did see it as a sin.
Jist as well 'cause today, how kin you Midgie Rake a Wheelie Bin.

Porridge.

You either loved it or ye loathed it, and that is the honest truth.
Loving each spoonful of it, or wanting to spit it oot yer mooth.

My sister sprinkled sugar over it, I thought she wid never halt.
While I was totally opposite, and over it I would sprinkle Salt.

I used to sit and watch my ol Ma, stirring oats into that big pot.
As soon as she poured it in my bowl, I ate all the blooming lot.

Winter morning's the porridge acted, just like Central Heating.
Weans that didn't eat porridge had faces that were aye greetin.

In summer months my Ma bought other cereals from the shop.
Either Corn flakes, or the wans that went Snap Crackle n Pop.

I have to say that I wiz glad when Winters came back, nae fibs.
As Ma would make once again, porridge that stuck to my ribs.

Ye kin buy porridge in packet's into the micro-wave it will go.
But it's not a patch on the stuff Ma made, aw those years ago.

Back In The Day.

I'll never forget oor teenager years, dead keen on the fashion news.
Burds hid Dusty Springfield beehive hair I had winklepicker shoes

I used Burton's to order my suit's, in those days I wiz slim and sleek.
When getting my wages on a Friday, I paid it aff at Ten Bob a week

Preparing for the dancing on a Friday, in front of the mirror I'd stare.
Using big dollop's of Brylcream, I would shape then comb mah hair.

A few swally's in the Sarry Heid but not too much otherwise I'd list.
Then o'er to the Barrowland, dancin with lassies aw doing the Twist.

And if I wiz lucky I'd get a lumber, fae a lassie who looked just right.
Efter the fitbaw in the afternoon, I met her fur a drink Saturday night.

Gaun to a pub wae live music, cheering on the band with not a shame.
Getting kisses and cuddles on the bus, as I took her back to her Hame.

Sunday I'd have a pint in a Hotel as pubs diddny open back in the day.
Noo I hiv nae hair, my dancing days are gone, the Pension is my pay.

The Tenement Windae.

Aw oor Tenement widae's had lots of uses, as I sit doon here n think.
My Da cleaning the kitchen windae, while sittin halfway in the sink.

Back in the 1950's nobody had fridge's , shopping daily by the hour.
Leavin milk overnight on the windae cill hoping it diddny turn sour.

Playing in the back court, ye shouted Ma throw's a jeely piece doon.
Up went the windae doon came the piece, you were over the Moon.

Ma and Da had a room and kitchen, with a coal bunker in the lobby.
The guy upstairs had a Dookit at his windae, pigeons wiz his hobby.

Kitchen windaes looked into the back court,middens always mingin.
A cushion under your elbow, it wiz the street side fur windae hingin.

Ma used a wee claes pole to hang some washing fae her windae cill.
The pole had a rope either side of it, claes pegged ,the idea was brill.

This all happened years ago, life in the Tenements era was fantastic.
I live in a sheltered home now, and the windaes made of pvc plastic.

Granny of Mine.

We remember oor Grannies, who'd break yer heart wae their smile.
My Ma's Ma wiz a Glesga girl, My Da's hailed fae the Emerald Isle.

Whatever part of Glasgow you came fae, your Granny wiz the best.
Oatlands in the Soo side, Northside, Eastside, or Govan in the West.

My Granny lived next close tae me, in an auld tenement single end.
Her knittin needles clicked every day, wiz nuthin she coodny mend.

If Ma wiz working Granny looked after ye, back n forward to school
Stoppin at the shop, buying you a penny dainty, aw it made ye drool

Back fae school Granny did windae hingin, it wiz her favourite treat.
As she kept a watchful eye on me and mah pals, playing in the street.

We remember our Grannies love for us aw, as we were all growin up.
Can ye remember her reading oor fortune, from tea leaves in the cup.

Sadly oor Grannies hiv gone, to Heaven's door they queued in a line.
Saint Peter took them in Pronto, saying I also had a Granny of mine.

Just For The Record.

Remember years ago, TV had top of the pops and Ready steady Go.
Radio Caroline had top - DJ's-Tony Blackburn and Emperor-Rosko.

I loved to listen to Radio Luxembourg and Sunday nights top twenty
Top twenty played backwards to number 1, music wiz fab and plenty

When Friday night's came and I got paid I was slaverin at the mooth
Aff to Lewis's Music Dept, listening to the hits in a wee record booth

Teenager's everywhere had transistor radios, music it wiz in the air
Twas the Swingin Sixties, the records were fab, we diddny hiv a care

Elvis wiz just oot of the US Army, still making aw the Lassies swoon.
The Space race started, Sputnik's and monkeys flying aroon the moon

Spending yer pocket money, buying an LP listening to it aw weekend
The Beatles / Rolling Stones and Dusty Springfield, were all the trend

The years moved on I got aulder, the music wizzny the same you see
Thank God I can relive my youth listening to oor pop sixties on a CD.

The Fair Fortnight.

For the last two weeks in July, most of Glasgow folks said goodbye.
Going away fur the Fair and hoping that the weather would stay dry.

Lots of soo-side people went to Rothesay or Dunoon wae a big smile.
While others went to Blackpool for two weeks along its Golden Mile.

Everyone seemed to be so happy , we had money and it wiz The Fair.
Ye cood go to Billy Butlins holiday camp, just opened up doon in Ayr.

Ma and Da took us aff to Saltcoats, we aw travelled there by the train.
Then a new thing called a package-holiday, took folks over tae Spain.

Changing your money to Pesetas, aff to Espana withoot even a ruffle.
Where you drank San Miguel aw night and done the soo-side shuffle.

Oh life wiz great fun for the Fair Fortnight, suntanned as dark as hide.
But all too soon it wiz over as we travelled back tae the auld soo-side.

Back to the auld sunny Oatlands, by boat, car, train, or even the Plane.
We knew we were aw back hame, 'cause it wiz lashing doon wae rain.

Back Court Singer.

To the tenements of the soo side my memory it longs to linger.
Listening to that man who was known as the back court singer.

He'd stand there all unshaven, with his auld Bunnet in his hand.
Singing his heart out and hoping, that soon a penny would land.

Some guy would lift his windae, shouting yer doing in my heid.
But a wumman next door took pity throwin doon a slice o breid.

Singin the Rose of Tralee, and ending up wae the Skye boat song.
His song list was endless in a voice a wee bit shaky but so strong.

So who was this man, and what had happened to him in his life?
Had he once been married, with lots of weans and a lovely Wife.

It was easy for some people to ignore him while letting out a sigh.
But there for the Grace of Our Lord, he could have been you or I.

And as we tell our Grandweans, with amazement they all do look.
Oor back court singer is always remembered, in oor History book.

Hoat Watter Bottle.

Winter times could be freezing, in the tenements of old.
As the windaes rattled with the wind it made ye so cold.

Sittin round the fireside while listening to the radio or tv.
You'd feel so very cosy, in fact as snug as a bug could be.

Then Ma would say it's time for bed and off ye would go.
And in an emergency ye knew, under the bed wiz the Po.

Earlier yer hot water bottle had been filled by Ma's hand.
Wrapping a jumper around it, to make yer bed feel grand.

First thing you did when in bed was touch it wae your feet.
But quickly drew them back because of that bloomin heat.

Then when yer feet wiz warm you cuddled the bottle tight.
And drifted off to slumber as winters stars shone so bright.

Now we have electric blankets central heatin at full throttle.
I'll never forget my tenement days and my hot watter bottle.

The Square Sausage.

Of aw the food I've ever eaten there's one that's my favourite meat.
People know it as the Lorne sausage it's so good it jist can't be beat.

Ye can have it with a full Scottish-breakfast a laying on your plate.
Beside your egg, beans, tottie scone yer square sausage looks great.

I left Glasgow years ago to live in London with aw its cafe's galore.
But when I ask fur it on a crusty roll, they hiddny heard of it before.

Aw the cafe owners said, we have link sausages that taste so grand.
Well to be fair to them aw I tried them, but the taste it was so bland.

World Wide I've tasted all kind of sausages, that leave me at a loss.
Always dreaming of the square sausage aw covered in broon sauce.

Each year I holiday back in the soo side it's great to be back Hame.
Leaving London far behind, their sausage's jist dont taste the same.

Great ti be back with my ain folk and that is the God's honest truth.
Dying to eat the square sausage, that has me "slaverin at the mooth".

Gaun tae the Dentist.

Dentist's all over the soo side, their names all filled me with dread.
Laying back in their chair terrified, wae that drill just over yer head.

He'd get his long handled mirror so to hiv a good look in yer mooth.
Saying there's nothing else fur it, I'll have to pull oot your bad tooth.

Clamping on that gas mask, told you to count back to ten real slow.
But the most I ever reached was seven then aff tae sleep I would go.

When you woke up you'd be a bit groggy, your heid a spinning roon.
Handing you a glass of pink mouthwash, ye'd spit oot in the spitoon.

Then the gas masks got replaced by a needle injected into your gum.
Half of your face t'was frozen, yer mooth wiz feelin pure dead numb.

If ye had a filling the drill hittin a nerve sent ye jumping up in the air.
With a scarf tied around your mooth, you ran doon that bloomin stair.

Now as I get nearer to seventy years old, every day I do get humbler.
Dentist's don't worry me, cause at night my denture's go in a tumbler.

Nae Mod Cons.

And now as I enter my Autumn years, my mind drifts back in a haze.
To the memory of oor Ma's+Grannys , who worked hard aw their days.

Whether you hailed fae the soo-side, Brigton or maybe sunny Govan.
There wiz nae mod cons like today, nae fridges or a micro wave oven.

Feeding the weans, gaun for the messages and millions of things to do.
Doin their best to make ends meet specially if their man wiz on the bru.

Nae washing machines or tumble dryers, life for them it wizzny dreamy.
Standing in a queue every week aw waiting for their turn of the steamie.

Nae stocking food in storage freezers they got the messages by the hour.
Placing the milk on the ootside windae ledge, hopin it widdny turn sour.

Sometimes usin the Pawn shop, to get us a dinner onto the kitchen table.
Takin their turn to wash the stairs prayin the weans grew up fit and able.

God Bless oor Ma's+Grannys, whackin a rug wae a wicker carpet beater.
Their Heavenly reward awaitin them a Gold medal presented by St Peter.

CHAPTER 2

Braehead St to Fauldhouse St
[west side]

Braehead St to Fauldhouse St [west side]

Let me take you on a tour of what we used to know as old Oatlands before the regeneration took place, let me take you street by street and see if you remember the places we grew up in as weans when the auld tenements were still standing and we knew everybody up our close and the closes next to that, back to a time when life seemed so less stressful as it is today and us as weans were loved unconditionally by our Parents, Grandparents and neighbours.

I will start with the Ritz picture hoose in Braehead st where we used to go as weans on a Saturday for the matinee show or early afternoon show of the latest film and we would stand up cheering on the goodies and booing the baddies, it was great for us Oatlands weans to let our imagination run riot and we actually became part of the film itself. An added bonus that always had us cheering more was when a cartoon was shown before the main movie and were all in fits laughing at the antics of Sylvester the cat and Tweety pie etc. Then when the film was over we would all pour into Braehead st and pretend to be riding a horse [if it was a cowboy film] holding an imaginary rein in one hand and skelping your backside to make your horse go faster to chase the baddies with your other hand. Or if the film had been about Robin Hood then all your wee pals were your merry men while any lassies there wanted to pretend to be maid Marion.

Now us weans got the picture hoose money from our Ma's, the entrance fee and a few pennies to get some sweeties from Frank and Angelina's shop nearby in Wolseley st beside the Glue Pot pub or Brown's newsagents in Rutherglen rd just beside Hurrel's pub. Can you remember what we used to do to get more money for sweeties, yes we got one of our gang to pay his entrance fee into the Ritz then make a bee-line to the fire exit door beside the toilets and kick the door open to let in all of us waiting outside. It was pandemonium all us weans would be running all over the hall with the usherette chasing us with her torch shining and she would shout out I know your Mammy and I'm gonny tell her, of course we all found seats but if the usherette asked you for your ticket you would get a ticket off one of the other weans who had legitimately came into the pictures. Happy days indeed and remember the era that I am personally talking about is in the 1950's when hardly anybody had a TV set and going to the pictures was a great day/night out.

Next to the Ritz picture hoose you had the plots or to give them their proper name the allotments but everybody called them the plots [they started off as the Albert gardens then later changed to the Caledonia gardens]. These plots were a joy for Oatlands people with green fingers and I always remember in the summer months that there was an open Fete day where the people had their produce to sell be it potatoes or cabbages, etc that they had grown, or some people grew flowers and they all had their produce on wee tables where you could buy them. It was such a clean and tidy place as the people took a great pride of their plots. I must say that the biggest joy for weans on the Fete day was a table that had bottles of ginger on it and you could buy a glass of ginger for a penny or two, I remember one day my wee Granny Hendry took me and there was this stall that was selling stalks of rhubarb and there was a wee bowel of sugar on the table so you could bite the rhubarb then dip the stalk into the sugar bowel which made it taste all the better although I have to say that after a couple of bites it became "stringy".

In those far off days like the Fete days summers always seemed to be so really hot and the sun melted the tarmacadam on some of the pavements, do you remember the tarmac that had all those wee white chippings in it and the tar seemed to stick to your sannies and your Ma would give you a belt on the lug as she had just whitewashed them that morning!!, yes Summers were really hot and winter times could be bloomin freezing and the tenement windaes used to rattle as you tried to drift off to sleep.

Now moving down Braehead st after the plots you came to the end of Braehead st and there was a big metal/wire gate which was a back entrance into the back of Dixons blazes but I never saw any lorries ever going in there, looking through this gate it was just barren land. Coming back up Braehead st we had St Bonaventures primary school or as we all called it Wee Bonnies, this was the teachers entrance and beside this you had a kind of "creche" where infants like myself were brought when they were about four or four and a half years old to try and get them prepared for school when they turned five years of age. I clearly remember a lady teacher called Miss Shirley, she was very nice and we would play and maybe do drawings with crayons and we always had small fold down camp beds where we used to have an afternoon nap [I must be going full circle as I'm seventy years old now and I find myself going for an afternoon nap again ha ha]. Of course when I was five years old I went to Wee Bonnies primary but I will talk about that later. It's funny but somethings seem to stay in your memory and I have great memories of my primary school.

Leaving Wee Bonnies and going further along Braehead st we a had a row of tenements, a pal of mine Louis Robinson lived in one of the closes and so did the Gallaghers, Dorran's, Lynnas families plus the Slowey family and a boy called Brian Morris who lived in number 69 Braehead st, when he was nine years old his family set off for Australia I know this as I have just started speaking to him on Facebook, what a great invention this internet business is eh. Of course in one of the close here lived the singer/showman Glen Daly who was once called "Mr Glasgow". Then next on the corner of Wolseley st and Braehead st we had the Glue Pot pub ran in the early 1960's by a Pat or Des McFadden and then later by Jimmy and Bridie Bonner, Andy their son went to Bonnies school and went to his Ma and Da's pub at dinner time and he spotted a few of Bonnies teachers in the bar, as Andy said life was much better with these teachers after he saw them in his parents pub.

Now continuing up Braehead st we came to the Wolseley st Gospel hall but we used to always call it " the band a hope " it was in here that a lady called Jenny Tarbet worked as a Sunday school teacher to the weans and "Auntie Jenny" lived on our landing opposite us in Fauldhouse st. I can honestly say that she was one of the nicest kindest people that I have ever met in my life. She used to "smuggle" my big sister Jeanette and me in there on a Sunday afternoon and we got glasses of ginger and ice buns or cakes while singing hymns. As we were of the Catholic faith our Parish Priest Father Gilmartin heard of this and other Catholic weans going into the band a hope and he went "bananas" so we stopped going in there [for a wee while anyway]. I know when the back of our tenement collapsed we moved out to South Nitshill and Jenny moved to Toryglen but my Ma and her kept in touch, in fact one time when I was up from London to visit my Ma and Da, Jenny happened to be visiting Ma's house and it really was great to see her again and I thanked her for being such a good person to my sister and me and all the other weans in Oatlands.

Next to the band a hope you had John McKintyres pawn shop or as we called it "John the Pawn" and many a dinner was put on the table with the money people got for pawning an object/item. In fact in some cases it was a weekly ritual to pawn Da's suit on a Monday morning and redeem it again on a Friday night when he had been paid that's just the way it was back in those days. I remember going into the pawn, well climbing up the stairs and squeezing into the narrow cubicle with my wee Granny and you always spoke in a whisper in case the person in the next cubicle heard you but we were all in the same boat really. Also when somebody wanted to pawn something they would wait till there was nobody they knew about in the street before going in or if they did see someone they recognised they would wait till the coast was clear. John McKintyre actually had a pawn shop in Logan st before he was offered these bigger premises in Braehead st and promptly moved there, he also had a shop just round the corner in Rutherglen rd which sold clothes that had not been redeemed from his pawn shop [as far as I know].

Moving on we had a painting and decorating firm called Sharpe's next to the pawn but back in those days of the 50's and 60's a lot of men were unemployed and done painting and decorating on the side just like my uncle Hughie Hendry who was very good at painting, it wasn't his trade but he was good with his hands, So I don't know if this Sharpe's firm had many contracts, I suppose they must have to justify having a shop there.

Then next to this we had Aldo's fish restaurant where you could sit down and have a fish tea or fish n chips take away, he ran this shop with his wife and his son who was also called Aldo. I remember standing in there one day and a girl called Jeanette Russell from 63

Wolseley st won the jackpot on the one armed bandit machine, she won ten shillings old money and she must have though she was a millionaire, fair play to her she treated everyone in Aldo's, I had a glass of ginger from her and other people had other things, yes money seemed to have value back in those days.

Hurrel's pub [formerly the Braehead bar] was next to Aldo's and always a busy wee pub, I made a visit to Hurrel's when I was of drinking age and I believe it was Patsy one of Gerry Hurrel's daughters who ran this pub. I went back to fulfill the promise that I had made to myself as an almost thirteen year old school boy that I would have a drink in all the pubs in Oatlands when I grew up, sadly I never had a drink in the Splash or Chancers but I did in the other ones otherwise I couldn't have lived with myself and now that they are all demolished and cast into the history book I have the satisfaction that I can say to myself that I did.

Going along Wolseley st from Braehead st we had the Glue Pot pub on the one side and next door to that was close number 12, this was the close that my pal Billy Harvie lived in, he was the class below me at Wee Bonnies school and a great football player, in fact he became captain of Wee Bonnies football team. With the collapse of our tenement and us moving out to south Nitshill Billy and me parted company and I never saw him again until 52 years later when we met on Facebook. We made a meet up in the Laurieston bar in Bridge st, Gorbals and what a reunion that day was, Billy and his lovely wife Liz came along and there were a few other new friends who also came along [who I had recently met on Facebook] What a trip we took down memory lane that day when Billy and me swapped stories of how we had got on in our lives since 1960 a great day and a few swallys too.

Next to Billy's close in Wolseley st you had Frank's newsagent shop, ran by him and his wife Angelina, Baltushla was Frank's surname [of Lithuanian descent] and his wife Angelina was Italian and what a great wee shop they ran, us weans could get our comics in there and jauries [marbles] for the boys while the lassies could buy scraps to put in their books, in fact it was more or less a wee general shop and you could buy fire-lighters for the coal fire, playing cards, fags, books, sweeties etc and remember in those days in the 50's you could buy a single fag for a penny and you were always give a match with it. Frank's shop always had a great window display at Christmas time with wee fairy lights flashing and bunting and wee father Christmas's and "snow" stuck on the inside of the window it really was a great wee shop and like lots of shops you could get things on "tick" until pay day. When we moved out to the new housing scheme in south Nitshill, I couldn't believe my eyes one evening as Frank had bought a wee mobile van which sold ice cream , bottles of ginger, fags, crisps etc it was great to see him again.

Now next to Frank's shop you had open land or "spare grun" as we called it, I only ever knew it as "spare grun" but while doing research for my book here I saw photos of a row of tenement houses where this "spare grun" was, so it looks like subsidence or some structural fault had been the cause for these tenements to be demolished which had happened to a few other tenements before. Then we had Alice street but I will come back to that later as we keep on our journey along Wolseley st towards Fauldhouse st. So after Alice st we had number 40 and 48 Wolseley st, in number 40, I had a few pals living there, Andrew West, Robert Fulton and his wee brother William who I used to play with as a wean, funnily enough I met up With Robert and his younger brother William at the first Oatlands reunion held in the Glencairn social club just a few years ago which was great. Now we come to number 48 the close my wee Granny and Granda Hendry lived in, Granny was my Ma's Ma and I was in and out of her single end every day, My wee Granny Hendry was like a surrogate mother to me while my own Ma was out working and this happened all over Oatlands to other weans as I'm sure you will agree. I liked nothing better to go up to my Granny's and she would make me a plate of broth and then she'd do a wee bit of windae hingin to catch up with any news [gossip] from the other neighbours. Other people living up Granny's close were Malky and Marion Davidson, Connie Beattie, Mick McLeavey and his son Ginger, the Brown family and the Workman family.

After my Granny's close you had the start of Fauldhouse st [west side] and on this corner low doon you had a Bookies shop, I never knew the name of it but I knew it was a bookies shop because my wee Granny used to do the cleaning in there in the mornings and when I was on school summer holidays my Granny took me in there and I was enthralled by the blackboard that the "marker" used to chalk the racing meeting horses up on and all the odds that were given. I knew this as they were still up on the blackboard when Granny did her cleaning and I could rub them all off with a duster but what really caught my eye as 5 or 6 year old wean was a great big snooker table in the middle of this bookmakers shop and although I was too young to lift the cue up it gave me great pleasure to push the balls along the table with my hand and guide them into the tables pockets. Nobody ever seems to remember this bookies shop when I mention it but it was definitely there.

Now on the other side of Wolseley st starting at the Gospel hall or band a hope as I say we called it, we had tenements going from the band a hope to Fauldhouse st, you had number 21 where a George Mullen lived, we never knew each other but must have past each other a thousand times in the street, I only got to know George from Facebook a few years ago and he told me that he now has retired and lives in Spain. Next close you had number [?] where my great pal John Docherty lived with his widowed mother from Donegal, "big Doc" as we called him was in my class at wee Bonnies and I clearly remember playing football one day at playtime in Bonnies school yard when Doc went in to tackle another boy and there was an awful "crack" Doc was laying on the ground shouting I've broken my leg and as sure as anything he had, the ambulance was called and Doc was taken away to the hospital. Of course when he came back to school he had a "stookie" on his leg and us weans took turns to write something on it.

Next close number was 51, where my pal Billy Graham lived up, you had a shop either side of it, first of all was a wee dairy's it was ran by a man called Bill and his understudy young Andy and I remember all the boys [and some lassies] from Big Bonnies school coming in and buying "a loose cigarette" or a single as they called it and then lighting up, standing there with leather jackets on and drainpipe trousers and trying to be like James Dean the film star or Elvis and lots of them wore studded belts and when having a fight would take the belts off and use them against the other guy they were fighting, they were bloody fearsome I can tell you. On the other side of the close you had Cathy the greengrocers shop and she was a lovely lady and like all shopkeepers in Oatlands of that era knew everybody by name and when people went into Cathy's shop or any other shop you caught up with the latest news. So when you went for the messages that's what you were actually doing, getting news messages from other people, people in other cities or countries go for groceries or go shopping but us Glaswegians go for the messages and when you think about it that's exactly what we done, there was the McFadden or McFaddyen family who lived low doon next to Cathy's shop and then you had Fauldhouse st.

Let me now take you back to Alice st, you had close numbers 3, where Isabel Horan lived then number 9 and 15 and it was up close 15 that my pal Brian Donnelly lived and another pal called Eamon Monaghan, in fact their kitchen windows looked directly onto My Ma and Da's kitchen window [in Fauldhouse st] next after that you had the Janitors house belonging to Big Bonnies school, the Janny's name was Mr Gibbons and he was a miserable person but his son Jim was a pal of mine, he was a great goalkeeper and because his Da was the Janny we were allowed into Big Bonnies schoolyard at night time and played football, well a two a side game of headers.

On the opposite side you had Wee Bonnies school and I always remember it with great affection, I remember when it was 1953 and the coronation of Queen Elizabeth II, I was five years old and everybody in our school [and schools everywhere] were given a great bit tin of chocolates. My favourite teacher was called Jimmy D'Arcy and he was a character, always cracking Jokes to us boys and girls in his class, I remember him telling us one day I have just found a way of getting into the Pitcture hoose without paying, everyone said how Sir and he said just walk in backwards and they will think you are going out!! Since I have started using Facebook about 6 years ago I have met up with Brian Donnelly, Eamon Monaghan, Geana McPike [Sweeney], Mitchel Crombie and Ann McCourt all from the same class of mine in Wee Bonnies, in fact Mitchell and Ann got married and I met them at an Oatlands reunion along with Eamon Monaghan and Brian and Geana I met up with in the Laurieston bar in Bridge st Gorbals for a drink and a trip doon memory lane. I know I keep saying it but isn't this internet Facebook a wonderful thing, in fact when I met up with Brian Donnelly he gave me our school class photo taken in 1953 when we were all five years old. I had never dreamed in a million years that I would have this photo and it has pride of place in my living room in south London where I now live, and now and again I walk over to it and say "well class mates how did your life go, good I hope, because mine was brilliant".

One last thing about wee Bonnies school and Mr Jimmy D'Arcy, I served my 5 year apprenticeship as a bricklayer and when I had finished my apprenticeship I was working on a building site out at Thornliebank with this other bricklayer called John, he asked me what school I went to and I said well wee Bonnies was my primary school, he asked me who my teacher was and I replied Jimmy D'Arcy. He said that's my brother, wow!! now the thing was John was going to meet his brother Jimmy in the town that Saturday for a drink before they went to see a football match and he asked me would I like to come along. Of course I did, we finished work on Saturday at noon and I met up with my old school teacher about twelve thirty and I was still calling him Sir!! we had a few pints and a lot of reminiscing , just shows you what a small world it is eh.

Sometimes in Alice st a man would come along in a pony and trap and he would take about twenty of us in the back of his trap and for a penny each he would take us for a ride all the way up Alice st turning left into Kilbride st and back down Fauldhouse st and all us weans would be shouting and laughing it was so exciting and the guy had made one shilling and eight pence in the old money [1/-8d]. He sometimes took weans in his pony and trap from Braehead st all the way along Wolseley st to Polmadie rd and then back to Braehead st again. I'm sure he must have done the same down the Rosebery st end of Oatlands, perhaps one of you reading my book can remember it?

I can remember standing at the top of Alice street in the late 1950's and looking over to Dixons blazes as we had been told that the big red brick chimney was going to be blown up with an explosive charge that day. There were loads of men and women all standing about and there was a policeman too. Dixons blazes had closed down in 1958 due to a recession so this had to be 1959 or '60. There was a big explosion and dust was everywhere and a big cheer went up when the chimney came down but the next day when we looked the chimney that we had saw every day was gone and with it was a part of Oatlands and Gorbals history too. I suppose that this was also part of the clean air act to rid the sky over Glasgow of the smoke and pollution that caused all those terrible fog/smog attacks we used to get.

Now just at the top of Alice st you turned left into Kilbride st but it was really only a dirt track [it never became a proper tarmacadam st until you went further along it and you came to Logan st] so we move along Kilbride st and turn down Fauldhouse st with Big Bonnies school to the left hand side, as we pass it at the top end we had the girls section of the school where my big sister Jeanette attended and another Oatlands girl I would like to mention is Rosemary McKee Robertson from Wolseley st. Rosemary left Oatlands to go to Australia years ago, we became Facebook friends and met up in London when she was back on holiday a few years ago.

Then we come to the boys section of Bonnies, when I was in Wee Bonnies I failed my eleven plus exam so went to Big Bonnies, the people who passed the eleven plus went to Holyrood senior secondary school up at Crosshill. I liked Big Bonnies it was a rough and tumble school and there were always fights in the playground mainly due to boys being in different gangs and wanting to prove their bravado. There was an "initiation ceremony" for new boys which was a six feet high wall surrounding the gable end of my tenement house, there were big wooden timbers propping up our gable end wall as the wall was bulging and in this space surrounding them was an area full of broken bricks and it was over this wall that I was thrown for my initiation to the school. When the older boys threw me over it I was in shock and quickly climbed up this six feet wall and back into the playground area with my knees shaking but pretended I was alright [I pretended to be tough and not lose face!!].

I remember some of the teachers there Mr Vaughan for English , we called him "Frankie" after the singer/entertainer Frankie Vaughan of the time, Mr McLaughlin for geography, Mr Morgan for Maths etc and Mr Berry was the headmaster with Mr Lee the deputy headmaster. This Mr Lee had the nickname of "scud Lee " he wouldn't give you the belt he scudded his knuckles off your head and it was bloomin sore, this wouldn't be tolerated nowadays but that's how it was back then and we were all tough soo-side boys so we never complained ha ha.

The boys toilets were always packed at break time as most boys were smoking cigarettes and you could hardly see for all the smoke, the teachers raided it trying to catch the boys who were smoking but there were other boys posted as sentry's and if the teachers did get in all the cigarettes were quickly thrown down the toilets, I would imagine that this happened in schools all over Glasgow and not only Bonnies. What made me laugh was that most of the teachers carrying out these "raids" were actually cigarette or pipe smokers themselves!!

Funny thing was when I started school here I was in the lowest class but after the first six months we had an exam and I was top of the class, so I was moved up to a higher class and six months later we had another exam and I was top of the class again. Mr Berry the headmaster told me that this had never happened before and told my Ma that he wanted me to be transferred to Holyrood senior secondary school. So that was me sent to Holyrood for my last three years of schooling learning French and getting homework to do. Although overall I must say whether I had stayed at Bonnies or went to Holyrood I would still have ended up doing my five year apprenticeship as a bricklayer!!

There were quite a few street gangs in the Gorbals and Oatlands and I would say lots of them attended big Bonnies school, in fact one night when we had been playing a game of football headers with Mr Gibbons the Janitor son Jim and Doc and Brian Donnelly Mr Gibbons called us all aside and said listen boys I want to show you something.

He took us into Mr Berry the headmaster's office and opened up a wooden chest it was full of knives, knuckle dusters, belts with spikes in it, and so many other weapons that had been confiscated from Big Bonnies boys. These gangs such as the Cumbie, Oatlands Young Hutchie etc were absolutely ferocious fighters and later on in my book I will discuss these gangs in my Topics chapter.

Also I think I have the honour of being the only boy ever to have had his tenement windae so close to Bonnies playground that at playtime after eating my play-piece I would shout up to my Ma's windae [if she wasn't working] and say aw Ma gonny throw me a piece on jam doon and right on cue wrapped up in bread paper came my piece to land at my feet. How many of us Oatlands weans have done this over the years and shouted up to our Ma's for a piece on jam? and didn't it taste magic!!

I must tell you this story as I think it's too good to leave out, about three months before I left for Holyrood school the teachers had picked out a few boys and girls for a summer school holiday exchange with a French school and I was one of the lucky ones to have been picked. My Ma paid all the money in the one go and even though I went to Holyrood I was still allowed to go to France with Bonnies school. We left the central station on the train to Dover then ferry and train to Versailles [just outside Paris] it was night time and there were twenty boys and twenty girls sitting in our train under the supervision of four teachers. I had just turned thirteen years of age and I was sitting in an aisle seat on the train and to my right hand side of the aisle sat a girl called Elizabeth.

Now we all started singing the pop hit song "Sailor" by Petula Clark when Elizabeth reached over and held my hand, I had never held a girls hand before as I thought it was "cissy" to do this but a feeling came over me that I had never experienced before, I didn't know what this feeling was but I know I liked it and Elizabeth and me held hands all night long. We had a great two weeks in France, seeing all the sights in Paris and then it was time to return to Glasgow. I was searching for Elizabeth on the train as I wanted to hold her hand again but to my sorrow found her holding another boys hand!! ah well I think this was an omen of what my life was going to be like later on with the ladies and it did turn out that way!! but ach that's life or as the French say "c'est la vie".

Right so still walking down Fauldhouse st, after Bonnies school was my close, number 40 Fauldhouse st and the strange thing was that our back court ground level was six feet lower than the pavement level outside, I could never work that out. There were two massive brick pillars, flying buttresses you call them and they were "shoring up " the back elevation of Wolseley st, so there must have been problems with subsidence over the years I would have thought. We had lovely neighbours up our close and I will just mention a few, "Aunty Jenny" Tarbet from the band a hope lived opposite us on our landing and right above our house was my uncle Willie Glasgow who was a bookies runner, uncle Willie never married and he never had electricity in his house, he had a gas mantle to give him light and an old fire range to heat his dinner up on. Next door to him in the middle single end was Andrew Ewing a very nice man and he had a great win on the football pools. He won about £150 which was a fortune back in those days, he got my Uncle Hughie to gut out his flat and redecorate it and repaint it. My uncle did a first class job and Andrew Ewing said I'm so happy with it but knowing my luck the hoose will fall down, very sadly Andrew or Mr Ewing as I called him was right and a month later the back of our tenement collapsed in December 1960 and we were all sent to different housing schemes. I will go into detail later in my book about when our building collapsed.

Next close to us was 32 Fauldhouse st and again I knew most of the people who lived there, there was one girl called Christine Boucher, her Da was a Jamaican man and her Ma a Glasgow girl. None of us had ever saw a black person before and Mr Boucher was a lovely man. I remember that weans in the street used to go up and touch Christine on the arm "for good luck" because of her lovely brown colour, we became great friends and actually she and her family also moved to the same street as us in south Nitshill which was brilliant.

Also my uncle Hughie and aunty Annie lived there with their six children in number 32 and I will never forget that Mary one of my six cousins was standing at the open fire place with her nylon nightie on and it caught fire. Mary was badly burned and rushed by ambulance to Hospital, sadly three days later my cousin Mary died she was only nine years old, a year older than me. As a wean I found it hard to comprehend that I would never see or play with her again. I still mention cousin Mary in my morning prayers, God watch over her.

Now going further down Fauldhouse st we cross over Wolseley st and we have two more closes before we reach Rutherglen rd, a pal of mine Billy Morton lived up the first close and in the next close lived a boy called Ian Davidson. I'll never forget one Christmas time all us boys got cowboy guns and hats from Santa but for some reason Ian had asked for a red Indian outfit , a feather headdress a plastic tomahawk and a wee plastic bow and arrow. Oh that poor lad was chased by all us boys with our cowboy guns an he must have been shot a hundred times over and more, two days later he never wore his red Indian outfit again I wonder why ha ha.

Now we have come to the end of the west side of Fauldhouse st and we turn into Rutherglen rd and all the many shops stretching from there to Braehead st, we'll will start off with the Rosebery bar at 614 Rutherglen rd, it was owned by a Robert Bowes but I only ever was in it once when I turned eighteen years of age and came back to have a pint in some of Oatlands pubs, I remember telling the barman I had grown up in Fauldhouse st and was on a trip that night just so I could say that I had a pint in there, then next door as far as I can remember there was a fish n chip shop, a Butchers shop either Holmes or Ingles, a second hand furniture shop, Cochranes, the Post Office ,Green Vale dairy, John MacKintyres clothes shop, Glendale's shoe shop and Brown's the Newsagents shop next to Hurrel's pub.

Right opposite all these shops was the Hutchesontown bowling green and I remember as a wean standing looking down on these men rolling a ball along the green and thinking this is what you must do when you're old then, I thought these men looked really old about fifty, well I know the feeling as I'm seventy myself now. I know they had a wee clubhouse there and I have heard nowadays it does a real good trade at the weekends for functions, perhaps one day if God spares me I might pop in there when I'm up in Glasgow on my holidays.

Author's summing up of Chapter 2:

Well Folks, here is a summing up of chapter 2, we covered the streets from Braehead st over to the west side of Fauldhouse st and everything else in between that including the Hutchiesontown bowling green.

One thing I didn't mention was the gas lamps in our streets, we had a gas lamp-lighter called Davie Jefferies who use to come along on his bicycle and light the gas lamps on our streets and up our closes. Of course we also had overhead electric street lights and when we played football at night time in the winter months in the streets these actually became our "floodlights" for all of us young budding football players.

Another thing I would like to point out is that when I mentioned the shops here in this chapter you may remember another name for one of the shops I have mentioned, over the years shops did change their names so one shop in the 50's could become a completely different shop in the 60's or 70's etc, so please forgive me if this happens.

I remember Brown's the newsagents beside Hurrel's pub used to give you "tick" for something you wanted to buy and in my case it was the Glasgow Celtic book which came out about 1958 time, it cost ten shillings in the old money and the newsagent had a little card for me behind his counter and I would pay it off at three-pence or sixpence a time until I had finally paid off the whole ten shillings and the book was mine to devour. Just the same I suppose as any other football mad young lad wanting to buy a book about Glasgow Rangers. John MacKintyres had a clothes shop a few doors along on Rutherglen rd and you could do the same thing for an item of clothing, choose the coat or suit you wanted and paid it up on your card and when you had the total amount paid the item became yours, of course as the years changed hire Purchase came into being and you actually got whatever you wanted [there and then] while paying it up. Or as it was nicknamed the "never never".

Of course there was a clause when you signed the hire purchase contract and that was you had to have a "guarantor" who gave their name that if you failed to pay off the remaining money owed then they would become liable to pay for it, which caused a lot of friendships to end [sadly].

We also covered the two Bonnies schools, Wee Bonnies and Big Bonnies, the end part of Dixons blazes and Kilbride st which as I mentioned was more or less a "dirt track" until we came to Logan st and it became a "proper street" with tarmacadam on it. Of course opposite Kilbride st you had a vast area of open space with just wild grass growing on it and then the railway line. Also in this vast wild-land area you had bomb craters where German bombers during World war 2 tried to bomb Dubb's engineering factory the other side of the railway lines and to the left Dixons blazes. As weans we used to climb through the metal railings that bordered off this waste land and we would go in adventure to play in these bomb craters. Sometimes in the hot summers some "bad boy" would put a match to this wild growing grass and set it ablaze and the fire brigade was called out to put the fire out.

"Scares of fires" in regards to the British Oxygen plant site which I will talk about later as we reach the streets chapter of my book including Polmadie rd. We also covered the three pubs Hurrel's, [Braehaed bar] the Glue Pot and the Rosebery bar and not forgetting the Wolseley Gospel hall [the band a hope] a few other smaller shops and the bookies shop on the corner of Fauldhouse st and Wolseley st, the Ritz, the Pawn and the plots.

Chapter 3

News Bits

News-bits

Richmond Park was opened in 1899, it was named after Sir David Richmond who was Lord Provost of Glasgow form 1896-1899, knighted by Queen Victoria in 1899 and Richmond park was named after him. When we all talk about Richmond park I suppose you're like me and really don't give it a second thought, so it's good to find out a wee bit about our local park and as I have been doing the research for my book I have learned a lot, see you're never too old to learn eh. Lol.

Paper-store fire.

A waste-paper store fire in Oatlands was last night destroyed by fire, the paper store bounded by Bilbao st, Kilbride st and Logan st was over 100.000 square feet in area. Flames leaped one hundred feet up in the air as firemen and appliances from every fire station in the city tackled the fire. It belonged to Easson brothers Ltd and employed seventy workers, the manager Mr James Easson said he knew of no alternative employment for the workers. The fire which is believed to have started in the upper floor of the two storey premises broke out as two employees at the store Mr Robert Dunn and Mrs Margaret Bulloch were working overtime on the ground floor. As soon as they heard the crackling of wood burning they ran into the street. Mr Dunn phoned the fire brigade on 999, this happened on March 12th 1958.

Wullie Scorgies shop.

When Clyde FC won the Scottish cup in 1958 Wullie [a fervent Clyde FC supporter] gave all the weans free toffee apples from his shop in Rosebery st, needless to say there was a big queue of weans outside Wullie's shop that day. Frank McLintock was a paper boy for Wullie.

Frank McClintock and Davie Holt both born and bred in Oatlands were two fine football players who played for Shawfield Juniors at Rosebery park [home ground in Toryglen st]. Of course Frank went on to fame with a succession of English clubs including Leicester, Arsenal and Queens park Rangers while Davie had great success starting with Queens park then Hearts and ending with playing for Partick Thistle.

The Pend.

Between Polmadie rd and Elmfoot street became a hive of activity for the Police when in 1969 Karen Doherty's brother Austin and his cousin got into a lock up/garage and found a load of old newspapers, they tried to sell them to people in the street. The newspapers were dated pre WW II but were in very good condition, the boys were asked where they got them from and so had to show where they came across them. Subsequently the police were called in and when the boys pointed to the lock up/garage it was found that there were old vintage cars there, the fire brigade was called in because the cars were covered in dirt and had to be washed down. These cars were in great condition with lovely red leather upholstered seats, the cars were not claimed by anyone so were taken away and were placed in a transport museum.

Ritz Picture hoose.

It was at night when a youth crashed thirty feet to the bottom of a narrow passage between the adjoining terrace houses. He was taken to the Victoria infirmary where he was x-rayed and detained with a broken arm and other body injuries. A policeman patrolling near the cinema at the corner of Braehead st and Caledonia rd saw a light flickering on the roof, he summoned assistance and within minutes CID officers joined him while other uniformed policemen cordoned off the block. The CID men went through the cinema and up onto the roof where they spied a dim figure, as they chased him across the roof he fell down below to the ground, this happened in 1952.

The Kay bridge.

A new pedestrian bridge across the river Clyde was opened by councillor Thomas Kay, convenor of Glasgow corporation after whom it was named. Costing £42.000 to build, it is the first pre-stressed concrete bridge to be authorised for Glasgow, it is 103 yards long x 12 feet wide and links Oatlands to Glasgow green. It was constructed by civil engineers firm of Melville, Dundas and Whitsun between 1954-5. There was a plaque mounted in the middle of the bridge to explain its name but it either fell off or was stolen within the first two weeks of the Kay bridge opening.

May Miler

May lived at close number 56 Cramond street then later moved to 21 Polmadie rd right above Cochrane's grocers shop. May and her two brothers Franny and John attended Wee Bonnies school, May and her husband Robert started their singing career in 1988 and have went from strength to strength appearing in many clubs and the cabaret scene.

The Sonny Pon.

People of my generation will remember the sonny pon or sandy pond to give it its proper name where weans like myself back in the day played in the sand with buckets and spades but it also doubled as a paddling pool. Sometimes back in the early 1950's I clearly remember the park-keeper or parkie as he was nicknamed bringing a turnkey into the middle of the sonny pon and turning it and slowly water would fill up and us weans could go paddling. Some people haven't heard of this but I know my good friend Martin Curran remembers this too.

The Silent Death.

In 1971 a small boy was knocked down and killed by a trolley bus in Rosebery street at its junction with Dalmeny st, a unit of the fire brigade was called to the scene to free the boy's body from under the bus. The dead boy was later named as James Rae of 145 Roseberry st, R.I.P.

An Unknown Hero.

Today two children were rescued by an unknown hero from their blazing home at 105 Wolseley street, he kicked in the door, clambered in and handed three year old John Hannah to another man standing outside. He was then told that there was another child in the house, the hero struggled through the smoke and flames and brought out two year old Anne Hannah to safety. He then ran upstairs to warn the other tenants of the fire with his face blackened and his hands burnt but then he disappeared, a hero even too modest to give his name. The children's mother Anna Hannah had gone upstairs to visit her sister in the same building. What a very non assuming person that man was and fair play to him.

Glen Daly.

Who of us remember "Mr Glasgow," as he was sometimes called, he lived at Toryglen street, close number 3 and 3 up on the top landing, He was the resident host at the Ashfield club in the north of the city for many years. His name in real life was Bartholomew, Francis, McCann, McGovern Dick but I think he must have thought you can't have that as a stage name so called himself Glen Daly.

The Devil's tree.

Who can ever forget that old gnarled and knotted tree on the pavement outside of the railings of Richmond park, of course legend had it that if you didn't spit at the tree when you passed by it you would be dragged into by the Devil from its roots or at least have bad luck for the rest of your life. Oh that poor tree was a sorry sight to see, of course just like the tenements that once stood in Oatlands it has now vanished into the history book but we will always remember it.

Momentos.

Linda Stephenson a friend of mine who used to live in close number 29 in Logan street has actually got a brick from her old building in Logan st and keeps it in her garden out in Rutherglen where she lives now, oh and has a wee Oatlands plaque that her daughter bought her and a painting of an auld tramcar with Oatlands as the destination on its heading, great momentos eh?

Demolition.

On the point of Richmond park I have to mention that before it became into being there were dwellings situated at the bottom end which would have been opposite of where the Wee Mill/Chancers pub stood. They were demolished to make way for the new park. This was prior to the parks opening in the year of 1899, of course as I write my book in 2018 there have been lots of changes made to Richmond park with houses being built on it and a lot of the trees have been felled and a new pub/restaurant called "Jenny Burn" has been built and opened.

Wolseley st school.

A friend of mine Shelia McCormack Knox attended Wolseley st school and said that when you sat the old eleven plus exam, if you were in the top half of the results you went to John st school over in Bridgeton but if you were in the bottom half then you went to Calder st school up in Govanhill. Shelia was in the top half of the eleven plus but wanted to go to Calder st as lots of her pals were going there. [Shelia the rebel ha ha] Anyway the headmaster/mistress tried to persuade her to go to John st but to no avail. Shelia now lives in Canada but posts and comments regularly on Oatlands memories Facebook site.

Deafy McGregors shop.

On the corner of Logan st and Rutherglen rd you had Deafy McGregors newsagents shop, we went in there as weans to buy sweeties but as he was deaf you had to shout so that he could hear you. Now he had an Alsation dog as a guard dog behind the counter and because you had to shout to be heard this started the dog barking and you had to shout all the louder, oh man what a pantomime. I still laugh at that now over sixty years later.

Petition.

A petition was signed by 800 people to get something done about the busy crossing at the gushet of Rutherglen rd/ Caledonia rd and Braehead st. A nine year old boy Daniel Russell of 600 Rutherglen rd died under the wheels of a lorry at this bust intersection in July 1962. I remember as a wean back in the 50's that a Policeman was always on traffic duty here. He used to stand in the middle of Rutherglen rd wearing a white coat so the oncoming traffic could see him and the motorists in turn could see him for directions, he used to keep that white coat in the police box [Dr Who's Tardis] nearby.

Brian Morris.

Who lived at close number 69 in Braehead st went to wee Bonnies school and in his class was Terry Dick the son of Glen Daly the entertainer, Brian left to emigrate to Australia way back in 1959 with his family when he was 9 years old and has just recently contacted me through Oatlands memories Facebook site so I'm glad to give his name a wee mention here.

Bill Hands.

Lived at close number 81 Toryglen st and like lots of other school weans from Toryglen st who attended Wolseley st school Bill used the pend [at Polmadie rd leading through to Elmfoot st as a short cut to school, I just wonder whoever reading this also used the pen[d] on a regular basis and smelled those lovely fresh baked rolls from the wee shop just inside the pen[d].

Children thrown from window.

It was around 5.30 pm on the wet afternoon of the 28th of March 1961 that a report of a child having fallen from a third storey window at 39 Toryglen street, Oatlands, Glasgow came through the ambulance radio to driver Jack Kirkland. He would later recall that accidents of this kind weren't particularly unusual at that time. He would tell a reporter in the 1980's: "accidents of that nature were common occurrences in those days, especially with the old fashioned windows". But it soon became apparent that this was no ordinary fall and this was no accident. Before the ambulance had even reached the scene, a second call came over the radio reporting that not one, but several children had fallen from the same window, as the emergency services fielded dozens of frantic calls from the public. Jack would later recall: "As we turned into Toryglen street we were confronted by a nightmare. There was frantic activity, police cars everywhere. The policemen were trying to clear a path for us through the shocked and horrified groups of people... Women in headscarves and aprons held each other and cried uncontrollably."

As the responders forced their way through the gathered crowd they were confronted by the sight of five young crumpled young bodies lying on the pavement. One of the bodies, four year old Marjorie Hughes, had died on impact and had been mercifully covered by a blanket by onlookers, but miraculously the other four children were still alive, though gravely injured., 45 year old James Haiming would tell reporters his memories of that day, he had just returned from work when he heard two sickening thuds outside his Toryglen street home.

He would recall I looked out and saw two kiddies lying there, "having rushed out into the street he saw another child plunging towards the pavement from the third storey window. I half caught him on my shoulder before he fell to the ground- but before I could do anything else I looked up and saw two more kiddies on the way down. I felt so helpless, there was nothing I could do".

As the paramedics attended to the four injured children, the story of that day's events began to emerge. It seemed that the children had been invited by a local woman to her top floor flat to look at a litter of puppies. But once the children had been invited in, the woman bolted the door, opened the window and began to throw the children one by one from the window. Once the children began to realise the reality of the situation, they tried to escape.

Neighbours hearing the commotion ran up the stairs and began trying to break the door down, while on the other side a sixth child, a young boy, desperately tried to unbolt the door. He would escape unharmed but suffered badly from shock.

The dead child was Marjorie Hughes [4] of 15 Toryglen street, and the four injured children, Francis Lennon [7] , his sister Margaret Lennon [5] also of 15 Toryglen street, Thomas Downie Devaney [4] and Daniel McNeill [5]. The woman was 37 year old Jean Barclay Waddell, a former hotel receptionist and short-hand typist, she was charged the following day with 1 count of murder and 4 counts of attempted murder in Glasgow's Sheriff Court. During her appearance she was said to have "bitten her lip but otherwise seemed composed". She would later be found insane and unfit to plead and was afterwards confined to Carstairs Psychiatric hospital.

It would later emerge that Waddell had suffered a complete mental breakdown following the breakup of her marriage to soldier Floyd Oakman. After the end of the second world war she entered a sanatorium to be treated for tuberculous, but while undergoing treatment she assaulted a nurse and was then transferred to a mental institution. She was said to have suffered delusions and paranoia , sometimes believing herself to be Empress of Japan, at other times convinced that she was carrying an illegitimate baby, or that the police were watching her.

It would also later emerge that she had been subject to electric shock treatment in an attempt to alleviate these symptoms. Afterwards she was said to be frightened of undergoing shock treatment again that she would tell people she would rather die, she would attempt suicide by overdose.

Crime writer David Leslie would say of the case "What would save Jean from being hung, as much of the public had called for it, was that by 1961 politicians and most of the public had lost the stomach for marching a female to the scaffold. She would later fall into anonymity and died in a care home in 2009 at the age of 86.

Up Oor close.

My name is Gary Taylor and I lived at 11 Granton st, Mr McCartney across our landing from us had a right scary dog, one night the lights went out up our close [which was a common occurrence back then] I managed to find my way up the close in the dark only to be met by his dog 3 stairs up and boy did I get a fright !!!. Mr and Mrs Lynch lived underneath us with Mary and I always seemed to get Mary into trouble when she played football with us wearing her good shoes. Across the landing from Mr and Mrs Lynch lived Donny Turner for a wee while, then the Burns family moved in, down the bottom of our close was Mr and Mrs McFadden and Mr Wallace with John and James.

Memories of my mother sitting at her window watching us play whatever game was "in" at the time, football one night, tennis another night and on and on, then we went building bogies consisting a plank of wood, a couple of pram wheels held on by tin cans with nails through them. Oh and also Michelle Findlay and Frances Leitch a right pair of tearaways over at number 12. Mr and Mrs Noble's family as well, never a dull moment and all good times.

Place the ball.

Retired train driver George Sutherland found himself on the right track when he won £1.000 cash on the "spot the ball " newspaper competition. George 51 said he would take his wife Agnes on a good holiday with the winnings. They lived in Rosyth street, this was in 1983. I wonder what the value of £1000 would be nowadays as I write my story.

Sulemans Newsagents.

For over fifteen years Sol had his newsagents shop at Rutherglen rd and during his time there saw he saw many generations of Oatlanders growing up around him. He still holds the many memories of the area there close to his heart. I believe that good people like Sol and the other shopkeepers that we knew should be thanked earnestly for looking after us all over the years

Giovanis chippy.

The days when we got a poke of chips and not a bag. *Elaine McNulty*

Buttered roll and fritters with brown sauce, haven't found anywhere else that can compare so far!!! I loved being allowed to walk down Rutherglen rd myself at night while someone watched me from the corner to go to buy pickles and some Irn Bru. What a treat.
Angela Miller

Best Pizza out, Loved Nan, Patsy, Ruth, Myra and Elsie they really were all so very nice. *Angela Gillies*

Chips were amazing. *Frances Leitch*

Little and Large.

Eddie Large of the Little and Large comedy duo [Sid Little and Eddie Large] was an Oatlands boy who lived in Oatlands until he was nine years old leaving with his family to go to live around the Manchester area in England.

The Malls Mire pub.

Actually this was Galbraith's grocers shop until the late 1950's when the pub was built on its original site.

Clyde FC.

Clyde were a brilliant wee football team in the 1950's throughout to the 1970's winning the Scottish cup in 1939, 1955 and 1958. Fervent Clyde supporter Wullie Scorgie [remember Wullie's shop in Roseberry st] had organised supporters coaches when Clyde were playing their away matches from Shawfield park and had sometime ten or twelve supporters coaches leave from outside his shop.

Ducksie frozen over.

Remember years ago when the Ducksie used to freeze over in Winter time, it was great for us weans as we could go ice skating on the frozen pond but we were always warned by our parents to be careful in case that the ice gave-way. One of those time the ice did give-way was back in 1952 and a child had to be rescued, her name was Norma Eccles and her aunt Marion Pettigrew lay flat on the ice to rescue her, she pulled her to safety. Norma was aged 4 and lived at 12 Wolseley street.

Families flee as wall collapses.

Twenty three families hurriedly quit their homes in Fauldhouse street, Oatlands today when a large section of the outside elevation of the tenement collapsed into the back-court. Most people grabbed a few possessions and shepherded their children away from the building where sinks and pipes had been exposed.

Families with children sought shelter in the homes of friends, the others stood in the street opposite their homes awaiting the master of works decision on the property, "Which was condemned before WW II". Then word came through- - no one would be allowed to return to their home, the property was repairable but the cost would be so high the corporation would have to decide whether to repair it or pull it down. In the meantime all the families would have to make their own arrangements for alternative accommodation, if the corporation decided not to repair the property they could apply for new homes on hardship grounds but after a further inspection it was decided to shore up the damaged wall immediately and it is hoped that this will be completed by tonight and that nearly all the families will then be allowed to return to their homes.

A man whose home was amongst the most seriously affected was at work unaware of what had happened, he is Mr Thomas Gillon who left shortly after seven o'clock for his work as a builder at Castlemilk. One of his neighbours, Mr Michael McAleavy [44] a labourer who lives on the ground floor of the next close to number 32, said – it was like an explosion and I thought that the whole building was coming down. One of the first to leave the building was Mr John Potts [35] a cleansing department worker who had just finished the night shift. There was a rumble and my eleven year old son Robert said that the chimney has fallen down but when we looked into the back-court and saw tons of rubble and clouds of dust we decided to get out immediately. Mr Potts, his wife Alice and other members of their family, eleven month old John and seven year old Alister went to a neighbour's house.

Most of the displaced families found refuge in the homes of relatives and friends but not them all. Standing shivering in the street Mrs Annie Hendry [37] who lives on a first floor house at 32 Fauldhouse street, said- I don't know where to go or what to do I have sent away three of my children to school and taken the other two to my mother in laws house round the corner but she only has a single end so I don't know what to do.

Author's note:

This was where I lived, my family lived at number 40 Fauldhouse st and this was only a few weeks before Christmas, in fact it happened on the 13th of December 1960 and in just under a month's time I would become thirteen years old, we were moved out to the new housing scheme of south Nitshill and I just never really liked it. I always knew that I belonged to the soo-side and hated leaving behind all my pals, neighbours and my wee Granny Hendry. I always kept going back to visit my Granny and pals. It was like my heart being ripped apart, I know that I would still leave Glasgow when I was 20 years old to build bricks in countries half way round the World but I dearly would have loved to have spent those 7 years until I was 20 and even today as a 70 year old man writing this book I still feel "cheated" of those 7 years of not staying in Oatlands but I can't change what did happen although it was a terrible feeling leaving the soo side just as I was about to become a teenager.

The lady mentioned at the end of the story Mrs Annie Hendry was my Uncle Hughie's wife, my Uncle Hughie being my Ma's brother all sadly now passed away same as my Ma , Da, Sister and Granny Hendry.

Bomb Explosion.

There was a bomb explosion during WW II at top of Logan st / Kilbride st and one person was killed with others being injured, the

German bombers were trying to bomb Dixons blazes but obviously missed Dixons blazes and hit the "new houses" instead.

Shawfield Park joke.

Clyde FC were playing Third Lanark one day at Shawfield and there was a great crowd there, all cheering on their team except for this one person who kept shouting out "kill everybody, kill everybody" anyway Clyde scored a goal, all the bully wee fans were cheering but this guy kept shouting out "kill everybody, kill everybody." Then Third Lanark scored the equaliser and all the Hi Hi fans were cheering but this guy kept on shouting out "kill everybody, kill everybody." This wee guy went up to him and said tell me pal who do you support, and the guy said nobody, my brother's an undertaker.

Chapter 4

Photos

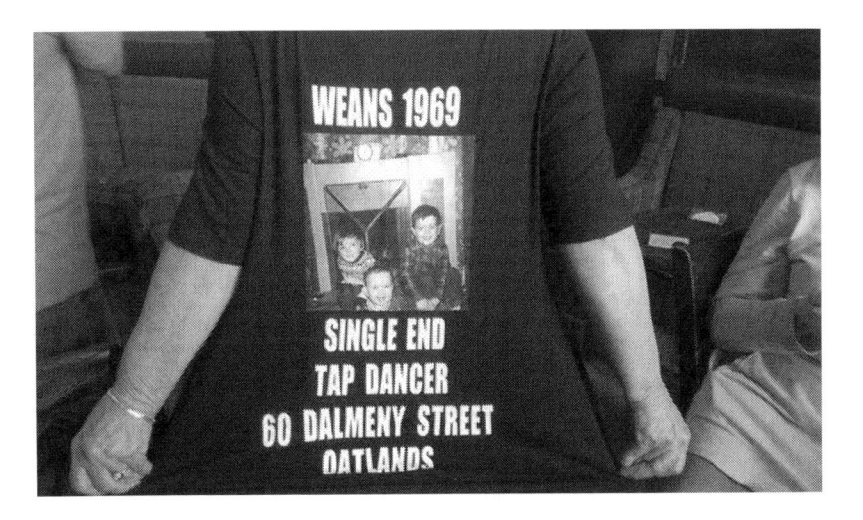

This Photo was taken by Christina Milarvie Quarrell [it's her wearing her Oatlands T shirt] way back in 1969 when she lived in a single end 3 up in Dalmeny st. Christina is a self- taught artist and an author who is also a poet, if anyone was interested in purchasing one of her books then you can send her a [PM] and for a donation to the Benny Lynch statue campaign she will get back to you.

I met Christina and she is a lovely down to earth person.

This photo is of 176 Wolseley street and is where my friend Jean Shreenan [Mullen] lived low doon with her parents, her next door neighbours were Jimmy and Betty Hobbin's. It was actually Betty who planted that lovely tree that you see in the photo. These "new houses" were built inbetween the war years of the 1920's and 1930's.

These "new houses" had inside bathrooms/ toilets unlike the old tenements where we used to have share a communal stair head landing toilet used by three families. Plus they had a front garden too.

A young Mother pushes her wean in the pram down Polmadie road, over to the left you can see the windows of the Polmadie locomotive engine sheds canteen. This was a bit of a steep climb walking up it as all of us school weans know and we walked it every day to school, come rain hail or shine.

In the background we can see the two chimneys of the "Clenny" Cleansing department incinerator and beyond that we had Hampden park the National football stadium. On big match days Polmadie rd could be jam packed with football fans either going to watch an international match or a cup final.

A photo of the "ducksie" frozen over I believe in the early 1940's, it was great when the pond froze over and us weans could go "sliding" along the top of the ice or some of the luckier ones had ice skates!! Of course some of the boys would make a toboggan and pull their pals along the ice.

When I was a wean growing up in Oatlands in the 1950's the duck pond used to freeze over quite a lot as the winters back then were really cold but the summers could be really hot.

Of course we had to be careful that the ice didn't break as we could fall in which happened a few times back then but us weans were fearless weren't we!!

A young Billy Scorgie outside of his Ma and Da's newsagents shop in Rosebery street, Billy's Da Wullie Scorgie was a fervent Clyde fc supporter and had between 10 or 12 coaches parked up outside his shop for Clyde's away matches. Wullie ran his shop with his wife Isa [sometimes called Tibbie] and their wire haired fox terrier "Shelia". He made the most wonderful mouth watering home made tablet.

In the 1950's Clyde twice won the Scottish cup and Wullie was given permission to display the Scottish cup in the front of his shop window for the day, now isn't that a great piece of Oatlands history eh!!

Wullie was also a gifted poet and had quite a lot of his poems printed up in the newspapers, his son Billy kindly sent me one of his Da's poems and I have put it into my Miscellaneous chapter for you to read.

This was the Glue pot pub that used to stand on the corner of Wolseley street and Braehead street, it was ran by Des McFadden in the early 60's and later by Jimmy Bonner and his wife Bridie in the late 60's early 70's. Their son Andy Bonner is a face book friend of mine. It looks like the pubs locals are all ready to go on a days coach journey from the pub.

If you look down the street a wee bit you will see the outline of the roof of Wee Bonnie primary school. I was 13 years old when I left Oatlands because the back elevation of our tenement had collapsed so I was too young to drink but I went back when I was a young man and had a pint in the Glue pot pub and a few other Oatlands pubs too.

A photo of the old "Kay bridge" which some people actually called the "white bridge" because of the concrete it was constructed of. This was a lifeline for Oatlands people who walked across it on a daily basis to get to where they were working. It was also used by many a school football team player on a Saturday morning, Glasgow green had numerous ash football pitches there.

Also who can forget walking over the Kay bridge to visit the "Shows" at the Glasgow fair time, there was always such a buzz of noise when the Shows were there and the nearer you got to it the louder the noise became, all the wurlitzers, motor bikes, dive bombers etc and your Ma and wee Granny could have their fortune told in one of the tents or play a game of "housey housey" while us weans were over the moon listening to all the pop records while eating a toffee apple.

What a place for entertainment, you could go and watch Clyde FC on a Saturday afternoon when they played their home matches and if you were a wean you could "get a lift o'er the gate" as men paying their turnstile money could lift "their son" over the turnstile and not have to pay for his entrance. Of course Shawfield stadium also had greyhound racing there on Tuseday and Friday nights and it always attracted big crowds.

Then sometimes you had a dance on Saturday nights in the Stadium's lounge area and many a good night was spent there having a drink and dancing to the live music band. There was also motor bike racing and sometimes you had pop stars like David Cassidy making live appearances inside the ground and a few boxing matches were also held there.

John the Pawn as John McKintyres pawn shop in Braehead street was affectionately known to us all, and many a time it helped put a dinner on the table. I remember going there with my wee Granny Hendry and sitting in the narrow cubicle, when Granny pawned whatever she had she always "whispered her name" in case the person in the next cubicle overheard her.

Just have a look at all the net curtains on the windows, brilliant white and all the windaes are very clean, we always pride ourselves in Oatlands for keeping clean houses inside and out. Next to the pawn you had the Wolseley street Gospel hall or as it was commonly known "the band a hope".

Going the other way you had Sharpes painter/ decorators shop and next to that was Aldo's fish n chip shop.

An Aerial view of the "Sonny pon" in Richmond park with Hutchesontown bowling green to the right hand side of it. Just look at all the shops we had on Rutherglen rd isn't it amazing. Oh and we can see the "hoat wa" in the background too.

Looking down Fauldhouse street opposite the steamie you can see a piece of "spare grun" and this is where my tenement once stood before the back elevation of it collapsed and it was demolished.

Getting back to the "sonny pon" I clearly remember back in the 1950's when the "Parkie" would use a turn key in the middle of it and it became a "paddling pool" what a great public park it was.

Chapter 5

Fauldhouse st [east] to Logan st.

Fauldhouse st [east] to Logan St.

So we now stand at the bottom of Fauldhouse st and we have a cobblers shop right at the corner which to my memory was always busy as lots of people back in the 1950's when I was growing up would have their shoes repaired, Re-soled etc whereas today it seems to be a throw-away society we live in. Also right outside the cobblers shop we had a guy called Wullie who had a fruit stall/barrow positioned there every day and he also seemed to do good business. Then as we walk along Fauldhouse st we had two close mouth entrances but I can't recall actually knowing anyone who lived up them except for a Mr Reid who on Guy Fawkes night would go into the back court there and let off a full box of fireworks, Catherine wheels, jumping jacks, squibs etc to the amazement of all us weans it was always a brilliant display.

Then we come to the corner of Wolseley st but carry on up Fauldhouse st and we come to the steamie, well what can we say that us Oatlanders don't know about the steamie, we first of all past by the big roller shutter doors which was the entrance for lorries to dump their loads of ashes/coal that would stoke up the furnaces [and once a week I would go in there and get a basin full of these ashes for our cat Dandy to use as her litter tray in our lobby] after that we came to the main entrance of the steamie where our Ma's and Grannies over the years took all their washing to be done, lots of women would take their washing in a pram and after "bumping" the pram down the tenement stairs, would wheel it all the way to do their weekly wash and if a woman lived in say Dalmeny street or Rosyth st then they had a bit of a journey but it had to be done because in those days we never had indoor washing machines like we take for granted in our kitchens or utility rooms nowadays.

Oh how those women sweated washing and drying their bundles of clothes and then wheeling them all the way home and bumping the pram all the way up the tenement stairs, I honestly mean this that all our Ma's and Grannies deserved a gold medal over the years for all they done to keep their families clothed and fed when money was not in great abundance and of course when the women done their weekly washing here they exchanged all the local news [gossip] it was like a weekly club for all the mothers to meet and if there was any scandal then low and behold the person who was getting talked about became "the talk of the steamie" and their ears must have been burning.

Of course the steamie had another function and that was the hot baths upstairs, the tenements never had inside baths or toilets and once a week people would take a trip for their hot bath, with me just living opposite the steamie I would cross over the street on a Friday from about the age of ten onwards [as I was getting too big to be washed in the sink or using the auld tin bath in front of the open coal fire] as my Ma had given me the money, I would pay downstairs at the main entrance, get my towel and bit of carbolic soap/towel then come out of there and turn right to the last entrance of the steamie and climb up the stairs and sit on a wooden bench until it was my turn in the queue for my bath. The guy who ran the hot bath for you would fill it up from the outside of your cubicle with a kind of turn-key. You would try and ease yourself into this big bath but the water always seemed to be burning hot, the guy would shout out once and once only, more hot or cold, I always asked for more cold but it was still too blooming hot.

As you were just relaxing and getting used to the water cooling there was a rap on your cubicle door which meant your time was up, so you stood up on a wooden duck board trying to dry yourself with the flimsy towel you had hired and when you did you felt really good. There was a brylcream unit on the wall and for a penny or was it two pennies? you got a dollop of brylcream for your hair, I never used it as I was too young back then but lots of men did and they would be rubbing it into their hair and combing it to try and look like Elvis.

Now moving past the steamie next door you had a wee bungalow type building which was a post-natal clinic for all the young Mothers who had recently had given birth and I remember there was always a lot of prams outside of this wee clinic and perhaps those same prams were used or borrowed to be used to put the weekly wash in them for women going to the steamie. As we pass by the clinic there were a few factory like sheds and they were fairly big, I think they were some sort of crucible works using steel for some purpose, anyway going past them we got to the top of Fauldhouse st/Kilbride st and here we had small bungalow prefabricated buildings that were actually an annexe to Big Bonnies school, I know as I had sat in one of them doing technical drawing and taught by a Mr Wylie, the other prefabs were for other purposes and the girls had one to do either needlework or maybe cooking lessons in. Then going along Kilbride st and as I say at this point Kilbride street was more or less just a dirt track [until it reached Logan st] we came to Bilbao st and going down Bilbao st we had a wee kind of mini industrial estate, I know over the years there was steel cuttings left out in the open and I always remembered looking at them and the rust all covering them when it rained perhaps this was part of the crucible woks too?, then further down Bilbao st we had a row of office type buildings but what they were I never knew but there was always a few private cars parked outside there which was unusual because in the 1950's there were hardly any cars in the streets where we lived in Oatlands.

Passing by that we came to a kind of scrap yard but it dealt in old motor cars which had been scrapped or was it a breakers yard? I do know before this it had been a yard for Tweedie the builders as my Da had told me that he once worked for Tweedie's and the men used to get picked up there in the mornings and driven to different building sites.

Then just after this we came to a piece of waste land or "spare grun" as it was commonly called by us all, it was here we used to play football matches and sometimes could end up 15 a side and believe me these matches were not for the faint hearted in fact if a referee had been in attendance then he would have ran out of red cards. There was no quarter asked for or given in these matches, it was all for pride and I remember when I was eleven or twelve years old playing in one of these rough and tumble matches and received a bad tackle, I got a bad cut on my leg and the dirt getting into didn't help, I couldn't stand up and the pain was bad but I never cried, ach you couldn't do that as you would be called a cissy, any way the game was stopped and a few of other players carried me all the way up to my house on the second landing, my Ma cleaned the cut in my leg and put some iodine on the cut well I almost screamed the house down but I managed to hobble to school the next morning see us soo-siders are made of tough stuff eh!!

Now just after the "spare grun" we came to the famous "hoat wa'" part of the steamie where us boys and girls stood with our hands behind our backs to get a heat from the furnace of the steamie, it was our meeting point and the ones of say eleven years old would listen in awe to the stories and tales coming from the older members of the "hoat wa'" gang. Of course the older members were trying to outdo each other and impress the younger crew with the elder boys also trying to impress the lassies but sure that was just part of growing up. I also remember just here was used when we played a game of kick the can, everybody caught would have to stand there in the street round the can waiting on somebody who was still "free" to come and kick the can and set all the captured prisoner ones free until the person who was doing the looking/searching got fed up and up would go the shout of "come oot, come oot wherever ye are, the games a bogie, the man's in the loaby I'm no playing" and the game would end, such wonderful games we all played while growing up, yes we sure did make our own adventure playground in our childhood in Oatlands.

Then opposite the hoat wa we had close number 63 Wolseley st and up this close lived Jeanette Russell, remember the girl who won the one armed jackpot in Aldo's fish and chip shop in Braehead st she lived up there with her family and pet Alsation dog Sheeba, also up there lived the Clancy family who later on in life would manage and run pubs in the soo side and later on in years to come I would walk into the Laurieston bar that they owned in Bridge st and low and behold there was John and James Clancy serving behind the bar after us not having seen each other for over half a century, I think it's called Kismet.

Now leaving number 63 behind we walk along Wolseley st and we come to Fullerton's an Ironmongers and they had a storeroom/warehouse here, it was quite a big place and my Ma used to do the cleaning in there twice a week, in the summer school holiday time I would go over there with my Ma and was amazed at all the different items that were stored in there from stepladders, mops and buckets, and shelves full of so many other household items. The

Fullerton's who owned this came from Muirend and had a big posh house and a front and back garden, I also went with my Ma there as she also cleaned their house and it was here for the first time in my life that I saw soft toilet paper in their bathroom.

Next door to Fullerton's warehouse/storeroom was a wee in-shot and in here was where Davie Kinghorn the milkman kept a stable for his horse and I remember quite a few times going in there to look at the horse which was kept in an open stable, also this area was used by Jesse Jackson the coalman, there were a row of what I think were lock ups and I know one guy used to keep his motor bike in one of these wee lock up places as I saw him at night times [after work] driving in there, opening one of the doors and parking it in there overnight.

Remember folks this was back in the 1950's and hardly anybody had a car in the streets unless it was a works van, that's why we could play in the streets and not have a fear of being knocked down but on Rutherglen rd it was a different kettle of fish as you had loads of traffic all day long. After leaving this wee set of lock ups you had another building /storeroom and I think it had something to do with storing ginger bottles [?] as I'm sure thinking back there were a few attempted burglaries into it at night time/early morning, I'm sorry I can't remember exactly what it was as I'm going back 60 years now.

Anyway leaving this building behind and going along Wolseley st you had another row of tenement houses and the first close was where a school friend of mine Peter Innes lived, he lived one up and his Ma used to always be doing a bit of "windae hingin" she was a nice woman and as I passed by I used to always shout up hello Mrs Innes as I passed by and she in return would always say hello Danny son, this is what I loved about living in Oatlands the friendliness of all the people, and if you ran a message for a neighbour you would most times get a penny from them for going for the message although your Ma would always say to you, don't you dare take money off of people for running a message but weans being weans we couldn't refuse the chance of a penny to buy a sweetie with could we Lol.

Along a few closes and we had a wee sweetie shop ran by a wee woman called Jeannie then next to that we had a bookies shop which I think was called Murphy's, it was at the corner of Wolseley st and Logan st with the door entrance in Logan st.

Now as we cross over the road and go back a wee bit we come to Bilbao st which had Wolseley st school a very fine solid looking building and a lot of my pals attended there like Billy Graham, Rab Fulton and his younger brother William, Robert Potts, who as I say were all pals of mine and then you had other pupils like Bill Hands from 81 Toryglen st and James "Jamie" McKenzie from 135 Roseberry st just to name a few and I'm sure that they and others all have a few story's to tell about their time there. I know that pupils all have a favourite teacher and Bill Hands told me he had a great teacher called Mrs McDonald and Colin Mackie tells me that he was thrown out of the music choir by teacher Mrs Christie's class for being over enthusiastic playing the triangle!!! Joseph Wilson told me he attended Wolseley st school from 1955-59 and had a lovely teacher named Miss Williamson, but an old battle-axe of a teacher called Miss Copeland who was a non smiler and I wonder if anyone reading my book remembers any of these teachers who were either really nice or the complete opposite. Miss Aird was a "dragon" as was Mrs Johnstone, while Mr Elder and Miss Neilson were both good teachers to their pupils.

Now I remember that at night time when school was over my wee pals and me would go to the boys playground area of Wolseley st school for a game of football = two a side headers and the playground just at the junction of Wolseley and Bilbao st was just the right size for the four of us as we tried to emulate or at least think we were the top players of the day whether we supported Celtic or Rangers or Clyde FC etc. I have to say that I thought that the "Janny" or to give him his proper title the school Janitor was a very fair man, he knew we were only in there for a game of football and so allowed us to stay but once he shouted right boys then that was it and we left the playground.

Now going along Bilbao st we had the same as the other side of the street, a lot of wee factory units and these included a saw mill and a timber yard over the years and an old used newspaper storehouse [which caught fire and I have explained about this earlier in my book] but to be truthful hardly anybody ever walked up or down Bilbao st except those who worked there and it was just always classed as a wee industrial estate with no importance really for anyone to talk about.

Then once again we reach Kilbride st and this old newspaper store continued till we got to Logan st and going down Logan st [west side] we had an ice factory and then Lawson's of Dyce [or Lawson's first before the ice factory? Or did Lawsons take over form the ice factory?] the sausage people and they would have long distance refrigerated lorries arriving at night time to load up or off load whatever the case may have been, I know some of the neighbours on the opposite side of the new louses in Logan st said they also came in the early hours of the morning and kept them awake or woke them up. Tricia Anderson I believe was one of them.

So passing further down this side of Logan st we come to M+M's chocolate/sweetie factory and people said that they could smell the sweets or chocolate smell in the air, right now we come once again to Wolseley st school and this time it's the girls side, now the thing was with Wolseley st school was the classes were all mixed, boys and girls together but they entered/left from different sides, so the girls entrance was in Logan st and the boys entrance was in Bilbao st. I'm sure that many women reading my book will remember when they attended the school and will have many fond memories [or maybe not so fond !!] I know that Colin Mackie's sister Jeanette McGregor loved going to the school and Myra Hall who lived opposite the school at number 35 Logan st used to wait till she heard the bell and ran across to stand in the line and Shelia McCormack Knox had a story to tell which I have already mentioned, oh and in the girls playground you had a Gym hall which I think was also used by other groups either as a gym or for meetings.

Now crossing over Wolseley st and continuing down Logan st [west side] we come to Murphy the bookmakers shop and I have to remember us again that way back in the 1950's it was actually illegal to place bets on inside a bookmakers shop, I know it sounds crazy nowadays but that is how it was back then and people of my generation know this as a fact. In fact there would be "bookies runners " who were men and they stood in tenement close entrances and took people bets off of them, write them their line out, take their money and go and place this and other peoples bets on in the bookmakers shop. Of course if that person's bet won then the bookies runner would pay them out their winnings in the same close entrance where they placed their bet on with him. There were quite a few times that the bookies shop was raided by the police and everybody standing in the bookies shop would be bundled into the Black Mariah or Paddy wagon and taken to Lawmoor st police station for illegal gathering, of course the bookie on hearing this would go to the police station and pay all of their fines which was probably about ten shillings each, but how crazy was this outdated law and thank God that it was stopped in 1960 or the very early 60's and people could go into a bookmakers shop in Glasgow and place a bet on a horse or greyhound without having the fear of being arrested. I mean just look at bookmakers shop nowadays as I write my book , you can go in sit down on a nice comfy chair , have cup of tea or coffee and a biscuit and watch all the races on television sets all over the bookies walls, and inside toilets for us all too.

Now we come to all the shops that stood on Rutherglen road, from Logan st to Fauldhouse st. First of all I will try my best to keep the shops in order the way that I remember them but please forgive me if I get them mixed up as we are talking about sixty years ago. We had Deafy McGregors newsagents shop on the corner of Logan st and Rutherglen rd and next was a fishmongers shop, then The Odd Spot restaurant, McCrimmons pet shop, [with the talkative mynah birds], a launderette, fruit shop, Doctor Camrass's surgery, Davidson's bakery, a Barbers, Climies Chemist shop, Frames the opticians and a cobblers shop right at the corner of Rutherglen rd and Fauldhouse st.

It was here just at the cobblers shop that you had a close where my school class mate Mitchell Crombie lived up with his Ma and Da, Mitchell lived one up if I remember correctly and sometimes when I was a wean I would go up to his house as his Da had a wee billiard table and the three of us would play a game or two, I thought this billiard table was fantastic, it was my introduction to the green baize and in later life I would become an ardent snooker fan going over the Toon to play in one of the many snooker halls in the city as did many other Oatlands lads. I am pleased to say that I met up with Mitchell at the first Oatlands reunion in the Glencairn club which was great.

I have to say that here on Rutherglen rd it was very busy with traffic back in the 1950's with trolley buses and commercial lorries and vans, you had to be careful if you were crossing the road. Although I must say that Sunday's were a very quiet day for traffic or when we used to get those terrible smog attacks, in the 50's they could really be "pea soupers" and the smog was that bad it seemed everybody had a scarf tied round their mouth to stop inhaling it, people of my generation will remember this well and the conductor of the bus's would walk in front of the bus shining a torch for the bus driver to follow after him. In fact the smog got that bad that sometimes the bus's or lorries would just draw into the side of the road and park up as you could hardly see in front of you, in fact some Oatlands people working over the Toon or further away would walk it all the way back home from their work place at night as the bus's could only crawl along at a snail's pace and it actually was quicker walking.

Of course all these smog attacks were caused by the smoke belching out of factories chimneys and our own tenement chimneys where we all used coal fires, later on the clean air act was passed in parliament in 1956, where smokeless fuel like coke etc was introduced to try and replace coal and slowly but surely over the years these smog attacks abated. Of course even when we did have smog attacks it did not deter all the budding young football players [including myself] from playing our game of fitba' in the street even though we could not see where the ball went when we kicked it, how's that for dedication eh!!

Right opposite my pal Mitchells' close was the start of Richmond park where you had a children's playground area where you had a paddling pond which later changed into a sand pit pond or the "sonny pon " as it was affectionately called, right at the start of the "sonny pon" and wedged in between it and the bowling green was an old red coloured street telephone box with the old A and B buttons, now my Da never drank or smoked and his hobby was electrics, tape recorders etc and we also had a landline phone in our house. I think we were the first people in our street or our area that had one but this was the mid-fifties and hardly anybody had a phone [except shopkeepers who had one in their shops] so nobody ever rang our house phone. Once a week my Da would give me four old pennies and I would have to go down our street, cross over Rutherglen rd to get to this phone box and ring my Da up, when he picked the phone up after me ringing our number he always said "hello who is it"!!! who did he think it was ha ha. was my Da having a laugh. Lol.

Of course nowadays not only do we have landline telephones in our homes but most of us have these smart phones that are with us 24/7 but back in those days phones were only used by shopkeepers or "toffs". Just like TV sets back in the fifties they were hardly heard of, in fact my Ma and Da bought a wee black and white TV set in 1954 when I was six years old and neighbours or people from streets away would knock on our tenement door and asked could they look at this new invention, it didn't have to be turned on, people just wanted to have a look at it to see what it looked like. TV back in those days were very basic with only one channel BBC 1, and hardly any TV shows in the morning or afternoons and night time viewing would end just after eleven o'clock at night, unless it was Ne'erday and the telly would stay on till half past twelve so we could welcome in the new year with Andy Stewart.

Of course today is totally different where we have TV 24/7 and all the sports and film channels etc but for most of us back in the fifties our entertainment was a night out at the Ritz picture hoose or for us weans the Saturday Matinee, my how times have Changed!!

Author's summing up of Chapter 5:

My summing up of Chapter 5, So we have took a walk down Fauldhouse st and past the steamie where there are so many stories to be told over the years of our Ma's and Granny's doing their weekly wash and their meeting place to catch up with all the gossip and news and if anyone had been misbehaving they would sure to have been the talk of the steamie!!!. We passed by the small post natal clinic [opposite big Bonnies school] then past the wee factories that took us to the top of Fauldhouse st/Kilbride st where there once stood three prefabs of big Bonnies school.

What I also have to say about this area between Fauldhouse and Bilbao st is at the top end there once was a football field/pitch according to an 1892 ordnance map and I have a faint recollection that a football team from st Francis Chapel in Cumberland st Gorbals used this pitch for their matches but of course with the passing of time it was done away with when big Bonnies school was built, then the prefabricated annexe units were built on where once stood this football field.

We also took a walk down Bilbao st with its mini industrial estate past by what once was Tweedie's builders yard and onto the "spare grun" where fierce tackling football matches took place. On a point of interest I was told by a friend of mine that this "spare grun" came about because it was bombed by German war planes during the second world war but I have looked at various ordnance maps up to 1933 and all it shows is vacant ground and it would seem very far-fetched if there were dwellings built here on say 1934 and six or seven years later flattened with German bombers as I cannot find any mention of this happening. I'm not saying my friend is wrong about German warplanes bombing the "spare grun" but according to the laws of probability it didn't happen and it was always "spare grun". Then we passed the "hoat wa" where once Oatlands weans big and small stood warming our backs and hands while telling story's to each other.

Then we went along the north side of Wolseley st passing by Fullerton's ironmongers warehouse/storeroom and the wee lock ups used by Davie Kinghorn and Jesse Jackson then onto wee Jeannie's sweet shop then Murphy's bookies shop at the corner of Wolseley st and Logan st, this bookies shop at a later date became a boys club ran by Wullie Mullan who I think came from Rosyth st. Of course we doubled back and went down the other side of Bilbao st where Wolseley st school boy's entrance was and the Janny's house stood, a few factory units and this took us up to the top of Kilbride st again. Earlier in the 1900's there was a saw mill and a big timber yard in Bilbao st but as I said before no one really took notice of this little mini industrial estate, it was just there but no one seemed to take interest in it except for the people going to work there.

We passed by the waste newspaper/storehouse/warehouse on Kilbride st and turned down Logan st [west side] passing the ice factory, Lawsons of Dyce sausage factory and M+M's sweetie factory before coming to the girls entrance to Wolseley st school, then crossing over Wolseley st we passed by Murphy's bookies then the cobblers shop with that overpowering smell of glue, dirty Peters shop and this took us to the end of Logan st.

Then we went along Rutherglen rd from Logan st to Fauldhouse st and all those shops, there really were so many shops in Oatlands when you come to think about it not like today where there aren't any or just a few that haven't been opened yet.

I clearly remember sitting in the Barbers shop way back in the late 1950's and the barber [was it Louis ?] had photos of Tony Curtis the movie star and Perry Como the singer as these were the haircuts that a lot of young men wanted at the time a "Tony Curtis" or a "Perry Como". I believe that this barbers closed down and moved along to just past the Piccadilly Café, some people will only remember Louis barbers at this position but I clearly remember sitting in his barber's chair before he moved. I also think at a later stage there was a ladies hairdressers shop, this may have been where the barbers once was? Also on the point of McCrimmons pet shop with the mynah birds I don't know if this shop was called Noh's Ark and Mr's McCrimmon owned it but a good few people have told me that there was a Noah's ark pet shop on Rutherglen rd. I though this Noahs Ark shop was down near towards Queensferry st end of Rutherglen rd but other people say no, so please forgive me if this is causing any confusion to you. Of course this Noah's ark pet shop could have been positioned on Rutherglen rd in the Hutchesontown area?

Now that is all the shops mentioned along Rutherglen rd between Logan and Fauldhouse st.

We also discussed the red coloured street pone box [which I will talk about as a topic in one of my coming chapters] and when I used to have to phone my Da up!!. The "Sonny pon" in Richmond park but I forgot to mention the devils tree opposite all these shops as I said earlier in my "news bits" chapter if you never spat at the devils tree as you passed by it you would have terrible luck, it was just a superstition but most of us done it including myself not that I'm superstitious myself touch wood ha ha. Then I briefly discussed those terrible smog attacks we used to have, our TV set and the neighbours wanting to have a look at this new invention and our nights out going to the Ritz picture house.

My next chapter, which is chapter 6 will be people telling their own stories about Oatlands and I'm sure that you will enjoy them as much as myself, I know I have said it before but I really think it is important for people to leave their stories behind for not only us to enjoy but for future generations to come after us to enjoy, so that they can see the way that we lived and how life was for us back in the day. If we don't leave our story's or if I didn't write this book mentioning people and shops and pubs etc then our Oatlands where we grew up in would/could be lost forever and that would be a tragedy because you know like me "God's little acre" was a tremendous place to live and grow up in and I'm truly proud that our book, yes it's our book , I may be the author but the book is all about us, all my life I've tried to be a man of the people, wanting to share what I had, so I want to share my book with you all.

This makes me both feel proud and humble at the same time too.

Chapter 6

Peoples Stories

Gerry Mcaleavy.

It was a day like any other, getting up for school and walking there. St John Bosco's new school was getting built then, and the old ground was used by workmen for all their machinery, dumper trucks, fork lift trucks etc and everyday as I walked by I would see men starting up the dumper truck which I had become quite fond of. I used to watch them start it up and then go about their business.

It was mainly Saturdays when I watched them and they really took my attention. I could stand there for ages fascinated looking at them while thinking to myself "I can drive that I know I can." One Saturday as usual I went down there and lo and behold there wasn't a sound coming from the workmen's area, just complete silence, which indicated for some reason that the men weren't working that day. Great!!

Now's my chance I thought, to have a go at this dumper truck. I got through the fencing alright and approached the truck with caution just in case a watchman was about but no, not one person was in sight, so I went over to the truck and by luck the starting handle was still in its position. I was eleven years old and this was my biggest adventure, I turned the starting handle phut, phut, phut and again nothing.

I tried a good few more times, each time more determined than the last, phut, phut, phut. Brrrrrrrr, Bingo it started and was running so I jumped in the driver's seat and took off while pressing all the handles to see how it worked, and the bucket was tipping up and down Brilliant. I drove around for a wee while in the workmen's area thinking I was Jackie Stewart the racing car driver lol.

Then I thought "I'm gonny take this thing down the street" so I crashed it through the fence, turning into Logan street, then turned left into Wolseley street. It was such a great feeling. I was actually driving this machine that I had dreamed of so many weeks before. As I drove down the street I slowed right down because there were weans playing who were only about five or seven years old and they were shouting out for a Hurl, so I wasn't going to disappoint them was I.

So I tipped the bucket down to let them step into it and once they were in I lifted the bucket up and on our merry way we went, turning into Elmfoot street then into Kilbride street and then back down Logan street with all the kids in the bucket. Then my Mum "big Joyce" appeared from a close and stopped the proceedings, making me lower the bucket down and letting the weans step out. She then asked had I crashed into the concrete on the fence and I said "No" and she said "you're a friggin liar because you were seen doing it" and she made me drive it back to where I had got it from.

The Police came to our house an hour later and cautioned me, and I was sent to a children's panel for my stupidity, which I now see with the help of hindsight but to us kids everything was an adventure and those weans in the bucket had a great adventure that day and I think they will always remember that day getting a ride in the dumper truck.

My punishment was being kept in for a week but I used to lock the bathroom door and climb out the window and climb down the drainpipe and into the street to play football with the rest of the boys. My Mum thought that I was up in my bedroom until she heard my voice in the street, then up the window would go and she'd be shouting at me to "get up the stairs smartish". I didn't listen to her and just carried on playing until my Dad whistled "Gerry up" so I then went up straight away but never once did he hit me, it was always "dae whit yer Maw tells ye." Aye right Da but I never did.

Author's note:

I met up with Gerry a few years ago and he is a larger than life character, actually he was getting married and he and his bride Irene sent a wedding invitation to me down in London and I traveled up by train for their happy occasion.

Alice McLaughlin.

I was brought up living in number 210 Wolseley street in Oatlands and around October 1967 when I was only five years old I was involved in an accident that made the front page headlines in the Daily Record newspaper.

"Oatlands girl saves baby brother".

I was told to wait at the bottom of the close mouth, or close as it was known to us with my wee baby brother who was ten months old and who was lying in his pram while my Mammy ran up the stairs of our tenement with her messages.

Being a very helpful wean I started bumping the go-chair up the stairs without her knowing. Halfway up the stairs, the stairs sky-light glass fell down and apparently I bent over the pram and saved my brother, a sheet of glass fell on my head while I held onto the pram.

I was taken to the Victoria hospital to get five stitches put in my head with blood covering my wee woollen suit, then the factor gave my Mammy a cheque for £25 as it was his responsibility to keep and maintain the building. There was a reporter from the Daily Record newspaper who asked me what I would do with the money and I answered saying I would buy wool and knitting needles to knit a new suit to replace the one ruined with all the blood from my head cut.

That tenement of ours was right above the Malls Mire pub on the corner of Wolseley street and Polmadie rd, and like most people we loved our house in Oatlands. I was the talk of the playground in my school which was Wolseley street school that had Logan street and Bilbao street either side of it.

My maiden name was Turner and back in those days I loved my school and living in the area while playing with all my pals at peever or skipping ropes etc, we had a terrific childhood back in those days.

Then when the Gorbals clearance started, Oatlands would follow and our part of Wolseley street was first to be demolished so we moved to the Dampies in Sandiefiels rd in the Gorbals although now I live in Cambuslang, but I will always remember when I made the headlines in the newspaper as a five year old, it's just a pity my mammy never kept the newspaper.

Author's note:

Yes sadly with the Gorbals clearance Oatlands would follow suit a few years later and people were displaced to different areas, most being the new housing schemes. When you look at the regeneration of Oatlands nowadays its nothing compared to what people of my generation knew it as. I think the new buildings are fine but to me it will never be a patch on the tenement area of Oatlands of old when we had that brilliant and very close knit community spirit.

I also have to say that every time I go back to Glasgow for a wee holiday break, I still am "gobsmacked" looking at all these new buildings when I go to visit Oatlands. In my mind I'm still trying to recall and place where the old streets used to stand. I get the bus going out to Rutherglen and it passes through Oatlands and when sitting in the bus I feel like standing up and shouting out loud to the other bus passengers " Hey this is where I used to live " sixty years ago.

Then all of a sudden the bus I'm traveling on reaches Shawfield stadium and I see the tail end of Richmond park and I think well thank God the park is still there but it has houses built on it !! And as I write my book a new pub/restaurant called "Jenny Burn" inside Richmond park has just opened too, definitely changed days all round eh.

Molly Dooley.

My first outstanding memoery as a child was starting School, it was my Da who took me. The Teacher appeared to be a giant, her name was Miss Heslin, my Da was five feet eight inches tall and Miss Heslin was taller than him, she wore nice shiny shoes, brogues they were and a dark red colour. For some reason I did not start at the usual intake date with the other five year olds and the term was already well on its way. Miss Heslin whispered to me that it was her first day too as she was taking over from a Miss McArtney. I was glad because Miss McArtney looked really old and because of her straight rigid back and the way she walked I felt fearful of her. She stayed for one week with Miss Heslin and I was right she was strict, putting children in the corner for talking or shouting and threatening to lock children in the cupboard.

My Da continued to take me to school before he started work, he was a docker and one wee boy said my Da looked like a tramp, I am assuming this was because of his work clothes, anyway I punched him around the ears and he ran away crying, so I got a letter and my Da had to go to speak to the teacher. That was the first of many letters.

When my Da's work shifts changed my big brother had to take me and they didn't want to be bothered with a daft wee lassie, so they tried to lose me, going through the back courts and over dykes and railings and they were amazed to find that I climbed and scrambled and dreeped aff dykes and kept up with them.

It was after school the real adventures began as they went over the Malls Mire and jumped over the burn, they played cowboys and the found "balloons" for me to play with and told me to blow them up, these "balloons" were smelly, I filled them up with dirty water from the burn and threw them at my brothers as they ran away laughing. Jack who was two years older than me was wounded and John found a blood stained rag and tied it round Jack's head, it had two wee strings at each end of it. Other times they would tie the blood stained rags onto branches to make flags. This is quite horrifying now, but that is how we played in the 1950's, I was eighteen years old before I learned what these balloons were, my husband to be had some, he told me he got them free with my engagement ring.

My brothers moved up to the big playground and continued going over the Malls Mire going up to railway carriages and goods wagons and nicking small packages being delivered from catalogues. I was making my own friendships by then, a big crowd of us all going whatever way, we heard shouts of " A Barney a Barney" and we would all run in that direction to watch boys fighting, no wrestling on the telly then, in fact no telly. I got kept in as I was told to keep away from fights. I climbed and done big jumps from dyke to dyke and climbed trees, made a rope swing while always getting injured. My mother who had ten boys at the time said she would rather have another ten boys than another one of me!!

Me and my pals pulled all the bins out of a midden [a bin shelter] and were making a den in a backcourt in Rutherglen rd when the whole shelter fell in on us. An ambulance and the fire brigade were called and there was five of us who were taken away to hospital, we were trapped under the debris and choking with all the dust. I got kept in as I had been warned about the dangers of these middens.

We were still in primary school when we would go into a midden in a back court and get boxes of sawdust and throw them over one and other and we would get tin tops from beer bottles in these middens and pry the cork from the back of them to make badges. We would cover our cardigans and jerseys with brightly coloured tin tops and do the back of our jumpers for each other. One evening we were doing this and a man was watching us, he said he knew a back court where there were hundreds of tin tops and he would take me and my pal there, we said we were going home as we were hungry, he then offered to buy us a poke of chips. Well instinct prevailed and I shouted to a woman at her window, her man and other young men came charging after him. They all chased him through the back courts jumping railings, they chased him from the back of the Braehead bar all the way up Oatlands and kicked his head in. Unfortunately by the time they got up to him it was the wrong guy, this guy was out looking for his dog. I got kept in again!!

I tried to behave and I would come straight home from school and say my prayers to Immaculate Mary and as I did not listen in school to prayers when they were being said, I was saying "Him I too late Mary" instead of immaculate Mary. My Ma really despaired for me so she told me to pray to my guardian angel where for " fold thy wings around me " I was saying "fold diamonds around me " and "Our father who farts in Heaven". My mother was in a tizzy, I never got kept in again, she was saying to my father that I did not even know the "Our Father" and he tried to teach me to say "Hallowed be thy name" and I would repeat "Hello what's your name." I was so much a pest.

I could go on and on, I remember when I got attacked in Florence street and fought off my attackers, my brothers saved a family who's house was on fire, the police brutality at the time, my Da losing a leg, how I became a good Catholic and still am. How my poor Mother not letting me go to Hollyrood senior secondary school because she couldn't afford the money for the uniform and all the neighbours in our street got together and got me my uniform, briefcase and beret from Black and Campbell's shop.

It doesn't matter where we came from, we enjoyed the journey.

Danny Gill.

I was born in the southern general hospital on 11th of January 1948 and was brought up in number 40 Fauldhouse street Oatlands [almost at the boundary where Oatlands ended and the Gorbals began in my view]. My Ma, Da and big sister Jeanette were living in number 2 Snowdon street Gorbals but when I was on the way, Ma and Da decided to move to Fauldhouse street as it was a bigger place - a room and kitchen in the tenements with no inside toilet and just like thousands of other people living in the tenements we shared a stair head landing toilet with all the other people who lived on our landing. There was something magic about the tenement buildings in the soo-side and we had this unbreakable close knit community spirit with everyone knowing each other and Granny's and Granda's and uncles and aunts all living close by or maybe only a few streets away.

Being born and brought up in Oatlands just a few years after the end of World war II, life was very austere for everybody and money was tight all around - I think that this is what brought us all together, we might not have had much but we did have we shared.

There were things like the "Menage" pronounced "Minauge" where our mothers paid in say two shillings and sixpence every week for say twelve weeks and then when it was their "turn" to collect the "menage" money your Ma would have money to buy her weans clothes or other essentials, and of course for us weans it was great as your Ma would always make a big fuss over you and buy some sweeties, so us weans loved that!!

It was the same when the gas man came to empty our gas meter, all the coins from the wee box where we dropped money into it was emptied onto the kitchen table and the gas man tallied up how much of a rebate your Ma was due and duly paid her rebate to her, once again us weans got a penny or two and we couldn't run down the stairs quick enough to get to the local sweetie shop to buy something from the penny tray.

In our street was the washhouse or as we called it the "steamie" where our Ma's and Granny's went to wash and dry all their laundry. It was very hard for our Mothers and Granny's but remember back then in the 1950's there were no such thing as a washing machine etc in our houses that we take for granted nowadays, and our Ma's would work like demons slaving away in this very hot steamie, then when it was all done they would pile all their washing into a pram and wheel it along the street until they came to their close mouth entrance to their tenement or close as we just called it .Once there they would then have to "bump" their pram with all the washing in it up the stairs until they came to their landing and their own door.

In addition in the steamie you had the hot baths upstairs, you paid for your hot bath downstairs and got your ticket, flimsy towel and a cake of carbolic soap [oh Lord even after all these years I can still smell that carbolic soap ha ha]. You went upstairs usually on a Friday afternoon/evening and sat on a bench until the man in charge would shout "next", then you would go into your wee cubicle and the guy had already poured hot water into your bath with a turnkey he used from outside of your cubicle. Once you were in the bath, this guy would then shout more hot or cold water, you always asked for cold as the water was piping hot, this guy would only ever ask you the once and if you asked for more cold water he just ignored you. Then it seems you were no sooner in your bath and a bang came on your door which meant your time was up , so you got out of the bath and stood on a kind of wooden duck-board drying yourself with the flimsy towel that you had hired but boy oh boy did you not half feel good. This made such a change, because when you were a wean your Ma would put you in the auld tin bath in front of the open coal fire, your Ma filled the tin bath up with boiling water from the kettle heated on the gas stove, if you had other siblings it was usually the oldest who went in first and the younger ones followed in turn. So it sure was a sign that you were getting older when your Ma gave you money to go and have a hot bath in the steamie.

All us weans played so many street games like kick the can, walking on stilts, rounder's, lassies playing peever/hopscotch or using skipping ropes while all of us boys played football from the moment we got out of school and sometimes it could end up fifteen or more a side, we all thought we were either Celtic or Rangers players or Clyde players as they had a great team in the 50's 60's and early 70's. These football matches could last for hours on end and how we loved them!

In those far off days we didn't have video games or laptops or smart phones as children of today have, we made our own entertainment in the streets and back courts of the tenements like "dreepin aff dykes" or jumping from one dyke to another, we were completely fearless and even if we did get a cut leg or fell off one of the dykes you were climbing you never cried as you would be called a "cissy". Of course we also played a game of "jaurries" [marbles] or one day we would go "midgie raking," and we could walk for ages visiting other people's midgies in their tenements and the ones we found to be lucky were the midgies up in Govanhill as it was rumoured that toffs lived there and often threw out lots of toys that were still in good condition into their middens.

I used to love going over to Richmond park on Rutherglen rd where you had a swing park, a rockery, a golf putting green, and a pond we called the "ducksie" where white swans swam and you could fish for "baggie minnie's"= wee tiny tadpole like fish. You could buy a cane – stick with a net at the end of it to catch these baggie minnie's from a shop on Rutherglen rd before you went into the "Richy" and you took an empty jam-jar from your house to put your baggie minnies in once you had caught them. Of course it was great if you did catch any of these tiny fish and you took them home but after a day of looking at them , you got fed up looking at them and they were poured from the jam jar down the kitchen sink or the stair head landing toilet. Not only weans from Oatlands visited the park but weans from the Gorbals and Bridgeton, this was our oasis and how we all loved going to the Richy. Later on some people would sail model boats in the pond and there were also small paddle boats [Pedlos] you could hire and enjoy yourself , what a place for us weans to go for the day.

I attended Wee Bonnies school [Saint Bonaventure's primary school] and to be truthful I never liked school that much, I just wanted to play football at playtime with my other school pals. We did however have a great teacher called Mr Jimmy D'Arcy who was always cracking jokes and one of the things that I always remember him saying was "right boys and girls what is the definition of the word "abundance" some of my class would say does it mean plenty of Sir? And Mr D'Arcy would reply no it means a Cookie doing the Cha-Cha. I left Wee Bonnies in 1959 and went to Big Bonnies junior secondary school just over the road from Wee Bonnies, but because I had achieved great exam results I was transferred onto Holyrood senior secondary school until I became fifteen years of age and left without any qualifications at all.

In the mid 1950's we had great music and I always remember us weans loving Bill Hayley and his comets singing "rock around the clock", then a new kid on the block called Elvis Presley appeared on the music scene and the music for us changed forever. I remember one summer night in the back court of the tenements in Rutherglen rd behind Hurrel's pub in the late 1950's and these lassies were holding a concert and standing on top of one of the concrete roofs of a midden or wash house and they were singing a Buddy Holly song "Oh boy" and they were brilliant, that memory has stayed with me all of my life, this was just another example of Oatlands weans making our own entertainment.

I would always go for the messages [shopping] to the shops for my Ma and if a Neighbour wanted a message I got them for them, they only had to ask and you gladly did it, sometimes they gave you a penny for running the message for them but your mammy always told you "don't you dare take money from neighbours for running a message" you would say "aye Ma" but the lure of getting a penny for a sweetie was too much to be denied ha ha.

In those days of the tenement shops, we bought our food on a daily basis as none of us in the 1950's had fridges to keep food stored in, and it was common practice to leave your milk bottle on the outside window sill overnight in the hope that it wouldn't curdle or fill the kitchen sink up with cold water and place the milk bottle in there. Your Ma would always take her turn of washing the stairs and all our windows and net curtains were pristine white, we might not have had much money but we prided ourselves in being clean honest people, and always showed respect for our elders, this has also stayed with me all of my life too.

As I have mentioned earlier in my book the back elevation of our tenement collapsed on the 13th of December 1960 when I was just a few weeks from my 13th birthday, it was due to bad maintenance and possibly subsidence and we were moved out to south Nitshill, a new housing scheme on the outskirts of Glasgow and I just never settled there, I'm not saying it was a bad place as I met and made new pals but I always felt that I belonged to the soo-side and was always getting the bus back there, south Nitshill as I say wasn't bad but it wasn't a patch on Oatlands where I had grown up with that close knit community spirit.

Before I left Oatlands as an almost thirteen year old teenager, I made myself a promise that I would return and have a beer when I was old enough in the pubs in Oatlands, well when I was old enough I kept my promise and had a drink in most of the pubs there, In Hurrel's , the Glue pot, the Roseberry bar and Logan bar and the Malls Mire, unfortunately I never visited the Splash or Chancers [Wee Mill] but a least I have the satisfaction that I can say I did have a drink in most of them as they are all gone now. When I visit Oatlands now on holiday it's either a pub in Gorbals or Rutherglen for a pint.

When I was 20 years old and after finishing my 5 year apprenticeship as a bricklayer, I left Glasgow in 1968 to build bricks in countries halfway round the World and never returned to Glasgow to live [sadly]. I did go back to see Ma and Da and my sister Jeanette on holidays but I never visited the soo side as I was only usually back for a weekend, then after Da passed away my Ma moved out to Bellshill so I had never really saw the soo side for almost 45 years.

My Ma then passed away and soon after my sister passed away too, so When I was 64 I said right I'm going to revisit where I was brought up, actually I got lost I walked along Ballater street and found myself passing by what used to be McNeil street library where I had first got my love for reading from and I saw the southern necropolis graveyard so I knew that I was on the right track. What a shock I was standing on Caledonia rd where the Ritz picture house should have been but it wasn't there!!

I looked over the way and saw Hutchesontown bowling green still there. So I crossed over and sat on the wee wall outside of it and looked over to where my street Fauldhouse street should have been but it wasn't there, there were new houses where the old tenements once stood and my old street was now called Fauldhouse way and I got a lump as big as a football in my throat thinking back to the old tenements where I had grown up with my Ma, Da, sister, Wee Granny Hendry and my Granda and all my pals and neighbours. It really was an emotional moment for me, I have only cried a few times in my life, like when Ma and Da passed away but I had tears in my eyes that morning. I thought back to all those memories and that close knit community we once had living there, yes we might not have had much money but what we had we shared. I always sum up living in those times as, "we had nothing but we had everything"

Author's note:

Since this time I now make trips back to the soo-side of Glasgow at least once a year to meet up with old friends that I have been reunited with through Facebook and newer friends too. I still get that buzz when I step off the train at the Central station.

Now I know this will sound daft but even though I know our old tenements are gone, every time I go back hame I still expect to see them, because those were the happiest years of my life and are in my blood.

Brian Donnelly.

I was born and lived in Oatlands. Throughout the 1950's and 60's I stayed in the old part of Oatlands which was run down, was unsanitary and had overcrowding housing but I have never regretted for one moment of my life living in the area.

As a child I had many friends who were from similar backgrounds, we all mixed and spent our free time outside, playing in all kinds of weather conditions, enjoying all kinds of games that were handed down from our parents to us. We were blessed with having a wonderful public park just across the road [Richmond park] which gave us endless opportunities to play. We were able to take a ball across the Kay bridge and play football for hours on end. We may not have appreciated it at the time but we had schools staffed with excellent teachers whose dedication was to equip us for the future. Due to most people in the area living similar lifestyles, materialism did not exist in our lives and everyone seemed to accept each other as equals and as children we learned to respect other people.

I have managed to live my life as a hard working individual with good old fashioned values, and now I look back on it and put some of my success down to being lucky enough to have been brought up in Oatlands.

Author's note:

When I started to learn how to use a computer about seven years ago, I came across Brian who was in my primary class at Wee Bonnies school and we met up a few years ago in Glasgow after not seeing each other for over 52 years. This was all down to Facebook, oh this internet is a great invention. We went for a drink at Georges square in a pub called the "Counting House" and we sat and had a good drink while swapping storyies of how we had both got on in our lives since our days of attending Wee Bonnies primary school. I have also met up with Brian on a few other occasions when I came back hame to Glasgow, a real nice down to earth person he is.

Isabel Horan.

I was born in Alice street in Oatlands and went to Wolseley street school which was only a few minutes' walk away from our single end, we had St Margarets Church and two schools which were St Bonaventures, [primary and junior secondary] and Wolseley street primary.

My first memories are of always playing in the back courts and streets and getting tar on my sand shoes [sannies] because in the long hot summer months the tarmacadam melted on the pavements. Little did we know when playing wee shops with a brick as the shop counter and raking midgies for goods to sell that we were learning our first social skills.

Then all our neighbours who were doing their "windae hingin" would watch over us as we were taking turns of playing skipping ropes or playing kick the can or maybe a game of peever. The rag and bone man would come round and would get old claes from our Ma's which we gladly gave to him in exchange for a balloon or maybe a whistle if you were lucky.

Richmond park was our very own paradise, the sand pit [sonny pon] the swings and not forgetting the ducksie. We would play there for hours until we were hungry, or perhaps we had taken a piece with margarine dipped in sugar, a milk bottle with water in it and a liquorice stick dipped into the water so it would become ginger Lol, ah pure bliss.

We had Rutherglen rd, our very own Argyle street with Chemists, cafes, Tunnock's sweetie shops, bookies , pubs, post office, a funeral parlour and a few fish and chip shops, newsagents etc. I always liked Frank and Angelina's newsagents shop just beside the Glue pot pub in Wolseley street and you could buy almost anything in there except clothes, and how I loved their window shop decorations at Christmas, it really was magical.

I moved out to Castlemilk in 1956/7 but my Wee Granny still stayed there in Alice street and I went back there to live with her, we sadly watched the demolition of the soo-side when they started to tear down our dear Oatlands bit by bit.

We owe so much to our parents and grandparents for bringing us up in that small but beautiful place called Oatlands, it was our own wee paradise. Even though I now live in Cumbernauld, my memories still go back to that magic time and place.

Chapter 7

Logan st [east] to Polmadie rd.

Logan st [east] to Polmadie rd.

Starting at the bottom of Logan st [east side] we had the Logan bar and a fair-sized pub too with a door entrance in Both Logan st and Polmadie rd, I had a few drinks in there in my late teens as my uncle Hughie and auntie Annie had moved back to Oatlands from another part of Glasgow and some weekends I would go and visit them and when I did I would have a drink in there. Also a workmate of mine back in the late 60's was called John Scott and he lived in the tenements above the bar, this was John's local pub but I never seemed to see him in there when I dropped in.

Along past the Logan bar you had a newsagents called McDougall's and I always remember it had a wee step up to its door, I remember that a new chocolate bar called "Caramac" seemed to be all the rage at the time in the late 1950's, it was a white chocolate but it was a bit too sickly tasting for me. My Ma used to give me school dinner money to go to the Odd Spot cafe/restaurant in Rutherglen rd but sometimes my school pals and me would spend it on sweeties instead, so we may have headed for the Odd Spot but lots of times we ended up in McDougalls or Jeannie Frenches sweet shop and I think a lot of people reading this book done the same when they were weans [don't tell my Ma!!]. Then on the corner of Logan st and Wolseley st we had the railway mission hall and I know my pal Shelia McCormack Knox used to use here as did lots of other Oatlands weans, in fact there was a another railway mission hall in Polmadie rd just beside Pat Fagan's bookmaker's shop.

So we cross over Wolseley st and we come to number 176 Wolseley st which was built at an angle between Wolseley st and Logan st, see it was hard to say what street it was in although it was classed as Wolseley st. Here another friend of mine Jean Mullen [maiden name] lived, she moved into these "new houses" that were built during the two world wars between 1920's and 30's with her family when she was one year old and left when she married in 1962 when her married name became Shreenan.

These were lovely wee houses and were two stories high, that was ground floor [or as we always said low doon] then 1st floor and 2nd floor being one floor shorter than the old tenements which were 3 stories high. People that moved in here found that they had a bathroom with a toilet and a bath, that was two things that we never had in the old tenements and who of you can remember the old stair-head landing toilets shared by three families and newspaper cut into wee squares hanging on a string and just a sink in your room and kitchen or single end but never the less that was our homes and I have to say that I loved the tenements. Anyway in Jean's house the neighbour's opposite were a couple called Jimmy and Betty Hobbin and it was Betty who planted a tree in the outside garden that was a lovely sight to see.

In fact all these "new houses" had wee gardens outside of them and some were kept beautifully by a person called Tommy Leonard originally from Gorbals, Tam was green fingered and quite a few people got him to attend to their gardens because of his gardening skills in fact I have inserted a photo of Tam at work in one of those gardens in my next chapter and even though Tam has passed on his memory will still stay alive with us.

Only thing Jean tells us is that the coal fire had to be kept lit most of the time to heat the boiler up for the bath and only one bath could be ran at a time and then it took a long time for the boiler to heat up again, so lots of people still went to the steamie in Fauldhouse st for a hot bath rather than wait for the boiler to heat up.

Now walking along up Logan st and past these "new houses" I have a confession to make which I have never told a soul before not even my Ma. It was in the late 1950's and I was aged about ten years old when I was playing in the street here with some pals when this woman lifted up her low doon window and said to me could I go a message for her, she said could I go to Toni's chippy in Wolseley st and get her a sixpenny poke of chips and a pickled onion, she gave me an old shilling piece and told me to buy myself a penny sweetie. Well off I went and got the chips and pickled onion and came back up Logan st chewing my penny dainty that I had bought. I went to what I though was her door but another lady came out and said no they are not for me, so I chapped on the opposite door and a man answered saying no not his either. I could have sworn that was the close, I waited in the street with the poke of chips stuffed up my jumper trying to keep them warm and wishing that the woman would open up her window but I waited and waited for ages but she never appeared. I felt very low within myself for not being able to give her the chips and her change, I waited a while longer then it was obvious for some reason the woman wasn't going to appear. So I walked up to Kilbride st on my way home to Fauldhouse st but left the poke of chips and the three and a halfpenny change on the ground, I knew someone would spot the money and take it but in my weans eyes I couldn't keep the money because to me that would have been stealing and this is the first time that I have ever told this story to anyone, I just hope that even today that the woman didn't think I had just taken her shilling and kept it without going to the chippy and I hope that one of the people's doors that I chapped on would have told her I had came back with her message.

Walking further along up Logan street and remember this is the same street where Gerry Macleavy drove the dumper truck full of weans before his Ma caught him, we come to the junction of Logan st /Kilbride st and remember it was here during the second world war just at this corner that the Germans dropped a bomb which exploded and killed a person, they had been aiming for Dixon's blazes which was helping the war effort with making iron / steel but obviously missed their target. In fact looking over from Kilbride st to the railway line and what would become a British oxygen company [BOC] plant, there were a few bomb craters that my pals and me used to play in, we would run around in circles till we got dizzy not fully understanding it was German bombs that had made these craters this was back in the early/mid 50's when my pals and me played in them.

Now taking a left turn from Kilbride st we turn into Elmfoot st and go down past all the gardens outside of the "new houses", I have a photo of a friend of mines sister standing in one of the gardens here at 16 Elmfoot st where her two Granny Connolly's lived, her name is Joan McAleavey and her sister my friend is called Frances McKinnon who was also born in Elmfoot st at close number 27, she moved later to

Toryglen but walked back every day to Oatlands to attend school, she used to cut through Jessie st to get to her home in Toryglen. So we know find ourselves at the bottom of Elmfoot st and we turn left and pass the few closes that take us back to Jean Shreenans house at 176.

Opposite there crossing the road we come again to the railway mission hall at the corner of Logan st/Wolseley st and walk along Wolseley st heading towards Polmadie rd, we had wee Jeannie Frenches shop where many a wean got a penny sweetie from, then passing by the old tenement buildings we come to close number 179 Wolseley st where Martin Curran lived for the first eighteen years of his life and John Bonner's shop was next close to him at number 189. Good thing about John's shop was that even after he had closed up his shop for the night you could still go to his close door chap on it, he would then go into the back and get you whatever you wanted. Martin's Granny and two aunts lived opposite at number 188 Wolseley st. Then after John Bonner's shop we had, Eastons dairy, Toni's chippy, a general store called Connetta, [later this became a bookies shop] and "We have it shop" then the Co-op on the corner. I'm not sure if all these shops were at the same time so one or more may have been at different years.

In relation to the "We have it" shop George "Geordie" Motherwell used to go to the cash and carry for the guy who owned it, and Geordie said there was a penny slot machine on the wall called "bonus" I think it had something to with red Indian chiefs faces on it and if you won the jackpot or Bonus then you got twelve old pennies, Geordie told me he won the jackpot a few times and felt like a millionaire, well at least back in those days money seemed to have value to it.

The Co-op on the corner of Polmadie rd and Wolseley st, if your Ma ever sent you for a message there, then what was the last thing she said to you before you left the house? "and don't forget my divvy number" it was a number that was imprinted in your brain and even today as I write my story as a 70 year old man I still remember my Ma's number. I loved going into the Co-op and watching that wee chute thing where the shop assistant took your money and placed it in this wee chute then pulled a lever and the chute on an overhead wire would zing its way up to the cashier above, who took the money and put the change due back into and zinged it back down to you or your Ma with your receipt in it. To the eyes of a wean this was like something out of "Flash Gordon" that we saw at the Saturday matinee at the Ritz picture hoose.

Then crossing over Wolseley st from the Co-op we had the Malls Mire Pub at number 210 Wolseley st [which used to be Galbraith's shop at one time], its first manager was Pat Harkins who later left to go and manage "The Beechwood" pub off of Aitkenhead rd, Bill Doaks was the proprietor of the Malls Mire, I'm afraid that this pub had a bit of a reputation for fights but it is not my intention to bring about any embarrassment to anybody or their families by saying people's names who drank in there, Ian Kennedy was the boss of it in the late 60's and early 70's and I remember as a wean when it opened back in the late 50's, of course I was too young to drink in it as I was only a wean but I did go back when I became a young man to have a beer in it, just so in later life that I could say that I had drank in it before it was demolished. I honestly wish that I would have had a drink in the Splash pub just round the corner in Polmadie rd but it's like a lot of things in life we wish we would have but didn't.

Then next door to the Malls Mire pub you had a few shops, Wullie Knox's dairy, a fruit and veg shop ran by John and Cathy Cunningham, this shop later became a scrap dealers shop and for a time was run by different people, Wullie Mullen was one and at another time a guy called "Henny". I can't remember if it was the fruit shop or Wullie Knox's dairy that was immediately after the Malls Mire pub so please forgive me if I have got them mixed up the wrong way round.

Then we now turn left up Elmfoot st and first close we come to was number seven I believe, and up on the first landing lived Frank McLintock the footballer who had a great playing career with English football teams like Arsenal and Queens Park Rangers, Frank in his youth was a paperboy for Wullie Scorgies newsagents shop in Rosebery st. He and another Oatlands footballer called Davie Holt played for Shawfield juniors at Rosebery park in Toryglen st. Davie played later for Hearts and Partick Thistle not bad for a couple of Oatlands boys eh!! Going along past the tenements where my pal Frances McKinnon [Mc Aleavey] lived at number 27 and then we come to the pen[d] which had the bakers shop selling hot rolls and where those vintage cars were found in a lock up.

Then we turn left again and we turn into Kilbride st and I always remember those two wee buildings I think they were a wee substation electric out buildings [?] and we now turn left into Polmadie rd and St Margaret's Church which saw many a wedding service and christenings etc over the years which I will mention in more detail in my Topics chapter, in fact later on there was a car repairs place that was beside St Margarets Church but I think the entrance was actually in Kilbride st. Anyway moving down Polmadie rd we come to the pen[d] which was used by so many people over the years as a short cut from Polmadie rd to Elmfoot st and the wee bakers just inside it selling those lovey hot rolls, next to that we had Cameo's newsagents shop where Ella the wife of the singer/showman Glen Daly worked, Cameos later changed its name to " the new penny" after decimalisation, and next to that was Scotts dairy and then the Splash pub which was run by husband and wife team Wullie and Madge Cowan. Most railway workers from Polmadie locomotive engine sheds drank in there and the Splash pub had beautiful stained glass windows etched with steam engine trains. May Sweeney Bishop told me that although she was too young to drink in there she would pop in and use their public phone as she only lived next close, in fact Geana, May and Barbara Sweeney lived with their brothers Martin, Billy and Thomas and Ma and Da Geana and Billy Sweeney in number 94 Polmadie rd, Geana, May and Barbara used to be known as the Sweeney girls to everyone and were always beautifully dressed. The Splash pub had a bar and lounge and a wee section where you could buy a carry out. Geordie Motherwell said it was quite a common thing mid week for guys to have a drink in there and/or the Malls Mire pub and at closing time which was ten o'clock back then, would walk up Polmadie rd to the Polmadie engine sheds canteen and get a great feed for under two shillings.

Then after the Splash pub you had the railway mission hall, Pat Fagans bookie shop, a fruit shop, Mario's chippy, Curries newsagents, wee Jeannie McCanns sweetie shop and the Malls Mire pub. Crossing over Wolseley st we come again to the Co-op shop and continuing down Polmadie rd we had a few other shops, Tommy the barbers, Vics bakery, Peter Skellons butchers shop and then finally Bonner's the chemist shop with all those large flagons/bottles of coloured liquid in them on the shelves.

Crossing over Rutherglen rd at this point took you to "the avenue" or "the drive" or "alleyway" as some people called it, you had the railings either side of you enclosing in Richmond park and you walked along here to get to the Kay bridge and crossing that took you to Glasgow greens football ash pitches where many a school football team played on Saturday mornings, I know that I played here for Wee Bonnies school football team on Saturday mornings back in the late 50's, I played as right back but I have to be honest and say that I was only a fair player but it was great just to get picked for your school team, and the notice with what players were picked to play in the team was pinned up in Wee Bonnies school notice board at Friday dinner time and seeing your own name there on it gave you such a thrill. The pitches were very hard, no grass at all jut black ash and if you got a cut on your leg you had to just grin and bear it. Also it seemed that all these football pitches were busy on Saturday mornings, everywhere you looked you saw different school teams wearing their colours and the referee was one of the school teachers who had to show impartiality!!!

Of course the other great event here on Glasgow green was in the summer time at the Glasgow fair when the "shows" came here and you could hear all the noise wafting over the river Clyde to the streets of Oatlands, and as you got nearer to the Kay bridge the noise and buzz of the shows got louder and then you were there walking through the shows the wurlitzers spinning around, the motor bikes going at full speed, everybody shouting, screaming and laughing it was pure magic and even if us weans never had any money it was just brilliant walking through the shows and looking at all the different stalls. Of course if you went with your Ma and Granny then they would want to go to the fortune tellers [a big queue outside the tent] or sit down for a game of "housey housey". My wee Granny's favourite stall was the one where you placed an old penny into a wooden chute and it rolled onto wee squares, if your penny landed inside a square with say the number 5 on it you got paid 5 old pennies from the guy inside the stall.

You spent hours upon hours here at the shows and every stall that you passed by would be playing all the pop songs of the day, there were a few gangs that would be walking about glaring at each other but you had a couple of cops walking about so the peace was usually kept. Then after being there for ages it was time to walk back to Oatlands but if you had money or you were with your parents they would buy you a toffee apple or a stick of candy floss or a poke of chips from one of the stalls and do you know what, all of the money in the world could not have made you any happier, oh how we all loved those days or nights going to the shows. Of course it wasn't only Oatlands people who went to the shows you had people walking from the Gorbals along Ballater st and crossing over the Kings bridge to get to the shows or people from Bridgeton walking there also.

Now coming back again over to Rutherglen rd again we had so many shops from Polmadie rd to Logan st and I will start with Bonner's the chemist and next to that was Hamilton's the newsagents shop, Miss Winks a kind of haberdashery, fruit and veg shop, Dr Gerber's surgery, the King's cafe, a laundromat self-service shop where Jean Shreenan's Ma and Liz Gilmour the boxing promoters wife both worked. Also a wee homemade sweetie shop then the Logan bar at the corner of Logan st/Rutherglen rd. I believe at some time there was also a Charles Kelly a painter and decorators shop and Tunnock's shop but I'm not too sure what years they were there, I've tried to give you the general picture of the shops layout but please forgive me if I'm wrong with any of them.

On the point of Dr Gerber, when I moved with my family out to south Nitshill our Doctor out there was also a Dr Gerber and to me he had very good looks and always dressed immaculately in fact he looked like a film star and a friend of mine Danny Sweeney from Oatlands said that the Dr Gerber he used on Rutherglen rd was the same, so I wonder, were they related? My doctor was along Rutherglen rd a wee bit, he was Dr Camrass and I hated going to visit the doctors, it just seemed an eerie place to be but it could have been worse it could have been the Dentists!!

As I previously mentioned my uncle Hughie and auntie Annie had moved back to Oatlands after being away in another part of Glasgow living and their children my cousins were young Hughie who would have been about 18 in the mid to late 60's and was quite a lad with the girls so I'm told, his brothers James and Donald [Donny] and sisters Anne and Martha. They all lived about the second close along from the Logan bar one up and they stayed there for a few years but I believed the moved out to Castlemilk or one of the other housing schemes and with me leaving to work in London and overseas from 1968 onwards we lost contact unfortunately, although before they left I heard that Young Shuggie broke a few girls hearts.

On my return from working in Australia after a few years in the mid 1970's,I went back to see my Ma and Da on holiday and treated them well as I had quite a lot of money earned from working in Oz and I got my Uncle Hughies address and took a taxi out to visit him and my auntie Annie and my cousins, I took my uncle Hughie out and bought him a good drink as I had returned from Austraila as I say with a fair bit of money, I also slipped my uncle and auntie a few quid too, my uncle Hughie was my favourite uncle but sadly he and my auntie Annie have sadly passed away now.

I also remember the boxing promoter Tommy Gilmour who lived up the first close beside the Logan bar in Polmadie rd, my Da was a boxing fanatic and he would phone up Tommy and say have you any spare tickets for the big fights on in Glasgow and if Tommy said yes then I had to walk round to his house and get them for my Da. At least that was one phone call my Da could make, for very few people in Oatlands at the time had a house phone as most people would rely on using the street phone boxes, remember the red painted ones with the A and B buttons.

Author's summing up of Chapter 7:

So now we have discussed the Logan bar which was formerly called Burnsides, McDougall's sweet shop and the railway mission hall in Logan st before crossing over Wolseley st and coming to the "new houses" where my friend Jean Shreenan [Mullen] lived and where I failed to deliver the poke of chips to that lady, then onto and up to Kilbride st where the world war two bomb exploded killing at least one poor person, going along Kilbride st and turning down Elmfoot st with the lovely wee gardens to one side of the "new houses" and on the other side the old tenements where Frank McLintock once lived. Then coming along Wolseley st, with wee Jeannie Frenches shop where weans would go daft just looking at her penny tray, then Johnny Bonners shop [that never closed ha ha] "We Have it" and Toni's great wee chippy and the Co-op, over the road the Malls Mire pub where there were a fair few punch ups, Cunningham's fruit shop later a scrap shop, Wullie Knox's dairy and then all the shops along Polmadie rd [west side] I think I left out the railway mission hall when mentioning all the others. I won't mention them again as there was so bloomin many of them!! But it does show you that Oatlands had so many shops in the area and look at it now hardly one!!

Of course and again we had all those many shops along Rutherglen rd, between Polmadie rd and Logan st, I do remember there was a wee step up to the Kings cafe, my big sister was about fifteen at the time and she used to go in there for a bottle of coca cola and listen to the juke box with all the rock n roll songs, I went in there too a few times myself when I was about twelve years old as I was starting to take a notice of girls lol.

Now across the road we had Richmond park and it was at this section of the park between Logan st and Polmadie rd that years ago back in 1892-4 there was a football ground called Braehead park, the home of Thistle football club and it had a grandstand too, although nothing was heard of them afterwards as far as I know, so there you are we had Clyde FC founded in 1877 and a few years later Thistle united and not forgetting the football ground between Fauldhouse st and Bilbao st which I discussed earlier,and also our own Rosebery park for Shawfield juniors, seems as we were just as mad about football back then as we are now Eh !!. On the point of the Braehead park where the Thistle football club played their ground actually became bowling greens later.

It's fascinating when you look back on Oatlands history and to think that before the tidal weir was erected downstream in 1901, Steamers would pass Oatlands on the Clyde, mainly from those built at Rutherglen boat yard.

Chapter 8

Photos

This is a photo of a very young Joan McAleavey in her Grannys garden in Elmfoot street she is the sister of a friend of mine who is Frances McKinnon. It was lovely for all the "new houses" built in between the war years to have gardens.

Frances lived opposite in the old tenements close number 27 Elmfoot street but moved up to Toryglen and she walked up and down Polmadie rd every day to attend school in Oatlands.

If you look down Elmfoot street you will see that some of the old tenements have been demolished in Wolseley street [just to the left of the shops] so this was the start of the beginning of the end of Oatlands as we all once knew it. Also where the shops are shown in Wolseley street is where my pal Martin Curran's close was. On the same side as the old tenements in Elmfoot st at the very first close entrance down at the Wolseley st end is where Frank McLintock the footballer stayed one up.

Another aerial view of the Steamie in Fauldhouse st, just back a bit we have Wee Bonnies primary school and Big Bonnies school both of them in Alice street. You have three prefabricated bungalow type buildings to the top right and these were the annexe buildings belonging to big Bonnies school.

To the right hand of the Steamie you have that small post natal clinic for young Mothers and their new born babies and next to that you have one of the factories in Fauldhouse st. And after them [just behind them] you have what used to be a mini industrial estate.

Of course we have Wolseley st school standing on its own at the corner of Wolseley st/Bilbao st and further on you see all the "new houses" in Logan st and to the extreme left of the photo we once again have a view of the "sonny pon" in Richmond park.

The "Plots" that one used to stand on Braehead st [with the southern necropolis graveyard at the very back of them]. Just look how tidy and neat that the way the sheds are all laid out. People back then took a great pride in their plots.

It was great in the summertime when the plots held an open "summer fete day" everybody would be selling whatever it was that they grew from cabbages to rhubarb to flowers. You took a stroll past everyone's little tables where their produce was on sale. I remember one of the little stalls sold ginger by the glass and us weans loved that.

Later on the plots and the Ritz picture house would be demolished and new flats [some for pensioners] would be built on where the plots once stood, so I think its good that we still have some photos to show what it was like before the flats were built and also to remind us of "Oatlands Once upon a time."

PS: Did you notice the three weans standing just in front of the gate?

Interior view of Oatlands Public Wash house circa 1950's.

"The Steamie" where our Mothers and Grannys sweated doing their weekly wash and the Steamie was right opposite my tenements close at 40 Fauldhouse st. What a difference nowadays when we have washing machines in our kitchens or utility rooms.

Women used to have to pile all their weekly wash into an old pram and wheel it from their tenement all the way to Fauldhouse st, of course they would have already "booked" up their washing time slot. Then they slaved away doing their washing and a bit of drying. There was many a good bit of "gossip" shared by all the women as they went about their chore and many an ear must have burning bright red. Lol.

Not forgetting that upstairs you could have a hot bath, paid for down at the window at street level, paying for your hot bath, towel and carbolic soap. You waited for your turn upstairs sitting on a bench, the bath was filled up for you and was always too hot. You would be just getting comfortable with the hot water when a knock on your cubicle door meant your time was up. Oh boy you felt a million dollars when you came out of your bath!!

A view of Chancers public house at the corner of Queensferry st/ Rutherglen rd, this was formerly known as the "Wee Mill" pub and was a great family pub with Dominoe nights, bingo nights and a sing song night.

Just look at the character and style of those magnificent red sandstone buildings weren't they magnificent.

Remember it was at this point when the old 101 trolley bus turned into Queensferry st and terminated and us boys waited patiently to try and get a "hudgie" off the trolley bus once it started off after the driver and conductor had their wee break. Of course the conductor knew what we were hanging about for and never let us get a "hudgie."

That stonework was the bridge over where "Jenny's burn" ran into Richmond park and then on its way to the river Clyde. With its water all different colours from the chemicals dumped into it from some factories nearby.

This is a photo of Tommy "Tam" Leonard who was a great gardener and tended quite a lot of peoples gardens in Oatlands he was very gifted. Tam actually came from the Gorbals but moved to Oatlands as his Ma and later his sister Cathy moved there. In fact he lived in 52 Rosebery st on the same landing as my good friend Jean Shreenan.

There has always been a "great movement" of people from Gorbals going to Oatlands and vice versa over the years.

Sadly Tommy Leonard is no longer with us but I thought it would be a nice gesture to post his photo here in the book so people who knew him could see him again and also that his name won't be forgotten in oor Oatlands memories.

What a lovely well tended garden, fair play to you Tommy and God Bless you.

Here is the pen[d] that ran from Polmadie rd to Elmfoot street and remember way back in the late 1960's when those cars were found in one of the old garages and the police were called in. It was one of Karen Doherty's brothers Austin and a cousin of his that found them. They were pre war cars and in very good condition and the last that was heard of them was that they were taken to a transport museum.

Of course over the years Oatlands people like Bill Hands would use it as a short cut going to Wolseley street school from his close in Toryglen street.

There was also a bakers just inside the pen [at Polmadie rd end] and everyone said what a lovely smell of freshly baked rolls met you first thing in the morning as you walked past the pen[d].

Another Facebook friend of mine lived more or less just above the pen[d] opening who is Paul Haggarty, who lived at close number 102 Polmadie rd.

**POLMADIE ROAD/
RUTHERGLEN ROAD,
OATLANDS**

The junction of Polmadie Rd/Rutherglen Rd, with Bonners the chemist right on the corner and next to it on the Rutherglen rd side was Hamiltons the newsagents shop and next to that was Miss Winks a "boutique" shop.

On the Polmadie Rd side we had Peter Skellons butchers shop which was rated very highly by people, at one time next to that used to be Vic's bakery [which I believe used to be Tommy's barber shop, or was it the other way about ?].

If you look at the photo just where Miss Winks shop was [up at the top] you will see that there had been a bit of demolition work done and as I have said before this was the start of the beginning of the end for the tenement era of Oatlands.

An aerial view where we see Rosebery park where Shawfield juniors used to play and wasn't it a nice wee park too. We can also see Toryglen st, Cramond st, Rosebery st, Dalmeny st and the "grey square" "part of" Dalmeny st, Granton st and Rosyth st.

Over in the background we can see Polmadie rd and St Margarets Church and nearer a few of the factories beside Rosebery park and it is when I personally look at photos like these then I feel at home because this was the era that I was brought up in as a wean although further along at Fauldhouse st.

As I have said in my book , I do think that Glasgow city council have done a very good job with the lay-out of houses in Oatlands as it is today but to me when I see old photos like this I know that this is the place where I would rather have lived.

Ritz Cinema.

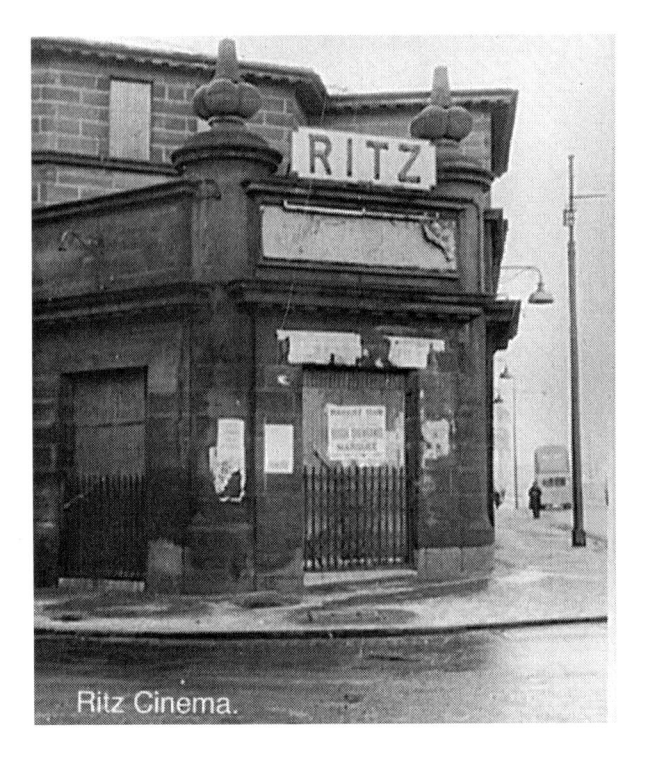

Well, what can we say about the Ritz picture hoose that hasn't been said before, it was our weans day on a Saturday morning / early afternoon and how we all loved sitting there enthralled by whatever film was showing. If it happened to be a cowboy film then we would pour out of the Ritz into Braehead street and pretend we were the "goodies" shooting the "baddies".

Of course this photo shows the Ritz in a state of decline, it was closed 1961 I believe but what memories it held for us boys and girls over the years and getting your entrance money form your Ma, of course she gave us a few penny's for sweeties which I usually bought out of Frank and Angelia's newsagents shop beside the Glue pot pub.

Yes sadly the Ritz has gone as have all the auld tenements too, but what memories for Oatlands people to think back on and all the money in the world could never replace our memories could it my friends.

Chapter 9

Topics

Oatlands Gangs.

John "Blue" Morrison has kindly allowed me to use his name and tell of his times in a few of Oatlands gangs, I'm not saying that the gangs were right or wrong or whether you liked them or not, but like John we both agree that they were a part of Oatlands history and should be documented. It's not my intention in my book to cause embarrassment to other gang members or their families so I will replace all of their names with a [X?].

John says he was a member of the Kay gang in Oatlands [taking its name from the Kay bridge] and a gang from Rutherglen stole from them, so the Kay gang went after them and got back all that was stolen using "persuasion". The Kay gang were active in the early 60's and had about twenty members in it, they fought against the Calton Tongs gang, Rutherglen young team. John was also in the Oatlands young Hutchie [OYH] alongside x?, x?, etc and many more and they would go looking for fights with Brigton teams.

They caught a few members of the Brigton teams and gave them a "doing". John's home was visited by the police on a few occasions relating to his involvement with the gangs he was in. One time the police came to his house and lifted him for fighting, then he was later sent to a remand home, but before this happened he was taken to his school and had to stand in front of all the school's pupils with the headmaster saying "that no good will come of boys who join gangs" but John has told me that "I personally made a lot of money" with being a gang member.

When John was sent to the remand home he met up with [X?] and they became life long friends.

PS.

One member of the Kay gang [X ?] was later charged with murder.

Polmadie Engine sheds.

These locomotive engine sheds gave a lot of work to men from all over Oatlands [and further afield] there were always plenty of steam engines in the sheds, some would be taken to the repair sheds to have work done on them, others would be "parked up" after say pulling coaches form London Euston and would be kept here until the return journey. Remember in these far of days of steam the coal tender of the locomotive had to be re-filled with coal for its next journey, then have its water tanks refilled too. I remember one night when I was about 14 years old [I was a train spotter at the time] that On a Friday night after school I would climb over the bridge on Polmadie rd and make my way down the grass bank and into the sheds to take the names and numbers of the locomotives and I came upon an uncle of mine James Glasgow, he was shovelling coal into this steam train to get it ready and I don't know who was more surprised him or me!!

When I was a schoolboy attending Hollyrood school a few class mates and me would use the Sheds canteen upstairs at school dinner time, it was really good food and cheap, we used it for a couple of months until one day a foreman from the sheds said you can't use this canteen anymore and I don't want to see your face anymore, so we were "barred" but I still went in there to get train names and numbers. Do you remember hanging over the bridge here with a steam engine passing by underneath and catching all the steam in your face, just things that us weans used to do. Then later on in life when I went down to London to work in the late 60's I always came back up from there about once every couple of months to see Ma and Da and I knew I was almost hame when my train from London Euston passed by Polmadie engine sheds on its way to the central station.

Rutherglen.

How many of us when we were weans walked to Rutherglen on a Saturday morning to see the pictures in the Rio or the Odeon, of course your Ma would give you your picture money and bus fare but we never got the bus , we just walked it as this would give us another penny or two for sweeties. To us it was all an adventure and remember where the boundary line was? Just outside Shawfield stadium, on one side of the sign it said Rutherglen and on the other side it said Glasgow, so we would stand with our legs astride, one foot in Glasgow and one foot in Rutherglen and saying to your wee pals "hey look at me I'm hauf in Glesga and hauf in Rutherglen" ha ha.

Of course the 101 trolley bus would have taken us into Rutherglen but we would rather have the bus fare for more sweeties as I said earlier, but the other bus the "red bus" that came from Glasgow Toon and also went to Rutherglen had a rule stating that if you boarded the red bus in the Toon, you couldn't get off of it until you had reached the Rutherglen boundary line at Shawfield which sounded daft and lots of people who wanted to get off at say Logan st would jump off the bus as it stopped to pick passengers up with the conductor shouting at you "you canny get aff the bus here." aye well too late pal. Lol.

In my late teen years I used to go to Rutherglen [which I thought was a great wee place] at weekend nights for a few beers and some of the pubs had live music in them, I remember going one night with my girlfriend Rena to the Viking pub and it had great music there. There was something nice walking up and down Main street in Rutherglen, with plenty of shops and I worked there quite a few times when I was serving my apprenticeship as a bricklayer. Now when I'm back in Glasgow on holidays I always try and go out to Rutherglen for a few hours and have a walk about, thinking back to when I was a wean going to the Rio or Odeon, and low and behold where the Rio used to stand and where I used to watch Saturday movies is now turned into a pub called "the picture house" which I think is a nice touch.

Old Phone boxes.

Do you remember the old red coloured red phone boxes that used to be in our streets in Oatlands, remember it had the old A and B buttons. You put your four old pennies into the box and phoned up your number, the phone the other end would ring out and if the person was in and answered then you would press button A and you would be connected and speak to the other person, of course if there was no answer then you would then press button B and your four pennies would come down the chute and you picked them up and left the phone box. Now I have to say that there were a few "bad boys about" and they would shove a bit of newspaper up the chute where the pennies dropped down, meaning if someone couldn't get connected and they pressed button B for their money back then nothing happened. That person would then storm off after having lost four pennies and this is when the "bad boys" who had been watching this would go into the phone box, pull down the bit of newspaper and Bingo!! The four pennies would slide down the chute and they would be off to the shop to buy some sweeties or maybe a few loose cigarettes [remember back in the 50's you could buy a loose cigarette from the shops and you would also be give a match to light it with]. This was back in the 50's and part of the 60's when most people never had phones in their houses or TV sets, there were a few phone boxes dotted around Oatlands and also in the old street police boxes you had an emergency phone flap that you could pull open and speak to the operator if you needed one of the emergency services. Of course today is all different with most people having these smart mobile phones.

If only our grandparents were about today and see these mobile phones that fitted into your pocket and also took photos and could tell you when your next bus was due well they just wouldn't believe it would they Eh!!

Saint Margaret's Church.

What a lovely Church this is/was and built by its own congregation no less way back in 1897- 1902, how many Oatlands people over the years went to St Margaret's for Church services there or got married or attend Marriages or christenings over the years, like Jim Campbell who married there, with his two sons being christened there also.

Jim Clark used to attend the life bouys while Margaret Tolmie was christened there and went to the rosebuds.

David Hodge's father was an elder there in St Margaret's in the late 60's and one day David went with him when the coal was being delivered and his Da had to shovel all the coal into the bunker on his own.

Evelyn McQuarrie attended Sunday school with her aunty Sandra, Evelyn got married there and her daughter was christened there too as was Sharon Mackin.

These were just a few of the names of people who attended St Margaret's over the years. It was a fine Hall and also over the years held many dances and social occasions and gatherings.

I just wonder over the years how many christening pieces were handed out to weans when Parents just had their baby christened there, remember the old tradition if the baby was a girl then the christening piece had to be handed to a boy and vice versa. I know at one time they had the Glasgow Caledonian band play there and the lead singer was none other than Lulu!!

It truly saddens me to see it laying there in a state of disrepair and although there has been talk of it becoming a community centre [?] as I write my book nothing concrete has been decided. This is one of the very last links tying us to that old era of Oatlands so let's hope St Margaret's can flourish once again in some capacity.

I must give a special mention about the Reverend Murray McGregor who was the minister in St Margaret's Church in the 1950's through to the 1970's he was a very well-liked Minister and would go out of his way to speak to everyone and make them feel at ease. God bless him.

The Hula Hoop craze.

In the late 1950's , early 60's we had a craze not only in Oatlands but all over Glasgow, do you remember it? It was this big wide plastic ring and you had to stand inside of it and try "to work it" up and down your body. It seemed the faster you twisted and gyrated your body then the longer this hula hoop would stop from falling on your kitchen floor or the ground if you were "hula hooping" outside with your pals. You broke out in a sweat trying to last the longest but it did make your head spin, this was in the summer months and then after a month or two this craze went as soon as it had came but I have to say it was fun while it lasted.

The Pawn.

Do you remember walking along to "John the pawn" in Braehead st, I remember it well as I used to go with my Wee Granny Hendry on a Monday. We used to climb up the stairs and then squeeze into one of the wee narrow cubicles, my Granny would place whatever it was she wanted to pawn on the counter and the assistant [always a woman if I remember correctly] would tell Granny how much she would get for it and when Granny said ok the assistant would ask for her name and address and Granny would always whisper it in case the person next cubicle would overhear it!!! It made me laugh to myself because when people were going to pawn something they would wait till there was nobody about in Braehead st that they knew, before diving into the close where the pawn was, if they did see somebody they knew they would just walk past the pawn until the coast was clear and double back. Nowadays with me living in south London I still see Pawn shops about but the difference being nowadays people walk in without there being any "stigma" being involved.

Really there was nothing to be ashamed about "pawning" something because it did put a meal on the table for the family when times were hard and of course when you had the money you would go back to the pawn with your wee ticket and redeem your article, there wasn't any social security about in those days like we have today so sometimes it was a matter of living from one week to another and re-pawning the same item on a weekly basis.

Of course sometimes people didn't have the money to redeem their article and when this happened and the pawn ticket was about to expire the person would sell their pawn ticket for half of the value, so the person who bought it got a bargain and the person who had pawned the article in the first place at least got some money back.

Yes times could really be hard back then but our Mothers always somehow managed to keep us fed and clothed, lots of times our Mothers would do cleaning in shops or schools to get some cash to keep their family going and how they done it was truly inspiring. No modern conveniences back then like micro wave ovens or washing machines or fridges/freezers that we all take for granted nowadays so between this and getting the pawn shop to keep their head above water took I think they all should have been given a medal.

Black and white TV sets.

Seems funny today but we just pick up the TV remote control and have the choice of so many many different channels to choose from like sports channels, Film channels, etc, but back in the 1950's when I was a wean hardly anybody had a TV set, my Ma and Da got a wee black and white TV set on hire from Stirling Hunters shop in Crown st and my Ma went there every Saturday morning to pay the weekly instalments off.

It was only a tiny wee set by today's standards but hey this was all new to us, if we wanted entertainment during the week it was usually a night out at the picture hoose. Then all of a sudden we had this new machine that brought to us programmes directly into our living room. Neighbours from streets away would come and knock on our tenement door just to have a look at this new invention, didn't matter if the set was switched on or off they just wanted to see what one looked like. This was us starting to come into the new age of technical development slowly but surely and when I look back nowadays I have to smile.

There weren't many programmes on in the morning or even the afternoon, it was mainly in the evening which started with the news then shows like panorama etc, but the weekends were special and I always remember on Friday nights at 7 o'clock we had Sergeant Bilko

[the Phil Silvers show] and on Saturday night we had a scary science fiction show called "Quatermass" which had us all enthralled and me a wee bit scared. This was TV in its infancy and later on we got ITV which actually showed adverts and yes you had a commercial break, which we thought was a brilliant idea, it meant you could run down the stair to the stairhead landing toilet and be back in time before the programme continued.

Later on we had the likes of Coronation street which was the first British soap, [as far as i know] not like today where you have loads of soaps but as I said this was us just starting to come of age and by the time the late 50's and into the 60's came lots of people had TV sets which was great but it was also the start of the death for the picture hooses and slowly but surely they started to close down with some of them becoming Bingo halls.

So today we can sit and have the choice of literally hundreds of channels to choose from to watch on TV but it all started back with that wee black and white TV set that Ma and Da hired from Stirling Hunters shop way back in the early 50's.

Saltcoats by the sea.

How many of us went away for the fair fortnight or a week down to Saltcoats for your summer holiday, it was great, the pure excitement of packing all the suitcases and getting ready to go over to the Toon and St Enoch's railways station to catch the steam engine train to Saltcoats and as the train pulled out of St Enochs's with the steam belching out of its funnel you felt like you were on top of the world.

Your Da had put all the suitcases on the overhead rack and you passed through the Gorbals on your way to the coast. Then you arrived at Saltcoats railways station and immediately could breathe in the sea air, oh what a feeling, then you all walked to your wee place where you were to stay for the next week or two.

As soon as you had unpacked you all went for a walk about the shops and took a walk along the shore then us weans could play in the sand on the beach while your Da tried to set up the beach deck chairs for him and your Ma. Lots of folks would paddle in the water while throwing the salt water on their face to try and get a sun tan. Sometimes you took your Granny with you too.

The joy of being bought a pokey hat ice cream and playing in the sand was pure magic and they even had a wee Shows down there, so again us weans would be spoiled getting rides on the different things like the hobby horses and maybe getting a stick of candy floss and at night times when you went with your Ma and Da for a walk along the promenade you'd be looking at all the boats laying on their sides that the fishermen would use and us trying to play on top of them.

It seemed every day the sun would shine [well maybe the odd wet day] and you made a beeline to the beach after Ma had made breakfast in the place you had rented and your parents always bumped into somebody they knew as it seems like half of Glasgow went to Saltcoats at the Glasgow fair, then on your way back to your place at night time Ma would buy you a poke of chips with plenty of salt and vinegar and this was just pure magic but all of a sudden it was time to go back to Oatlands and you couldn't wait to tell all your wee pals who unfortunately couldn't get away about the great time you had there. Your Ma always made sure that you brought back a stick of Saltcoats rock for them [remember it had Saltcoats written all the way through it].

Oh what a place and what a great holiday, although some other people went to other places like Rothesay or Dunoon or the like, it was great getting away but at the same time it was great to becoming back hame to your tenement and playing all your street games again.

Midgie rakin.

Oh yes, we all done it [well most of us] and it was surprising what "luxies" you found in the old open middens, the speciality to look out for was ginger bottles or beer bottles because at the time there was a penny or two deposit paid on them when they were bought, all you had to do was wash them with some water and take them to the shop or off license department of the pub. Some of the shopkeepers could become a wee bit funny and say this bottle wasn't bought here and you would have to make a trip round a few shops till you found one who would accept them, and give you the money for them, which you immediately spent on sweeties.

In some other middens you would find a toy that someone had chucked out but to you it was in good condition, you could spend a whole day midgie rakin [in the school summer holidays] going from one back court to another and when you went back up to your house your Ma would be screaming at you " look at you, your covered in ashes ," have you been midgie rakin again ? And of course you would say "naw no me Ma ". Of course health and safety would go bananas if this happened today but back in those days this was all adventure to us and in the school summer holidays we would have a new adventure every day, and as I look back now we had the most wonderful childhood growing up back then and I truly feel sorry for the children of today who will never experience what we did when we were weans all those years ago. We never needed any video games or computers back then for our enjoyment, our enjoyment was playing kick the can, rounders, kick-door-run-fast, street fitbaw, peever, etc and all the other games that brought us joy, then going back to our tenement house at night time manky dirty but happy.

Lighting the fire.

Now here is an art form that has sadly died away over the the years, remember how we used to get the old open coal fire lit?, we would get a sheet of newspaper and crumple it up and lay it on top of the grate and put a couple of wee bits of coal on it [not too many] and then build a few sticks of wood, like a red Indian teepee so plenty of air could pass through. We would get a match and light the crumpled newspaper so it would light the bits of wood and in turn set light to the coal lumps.

Of course we had to help it along and we would be down on our knees blowing wind from our cheeks till we thought we would go dizzy to help the fire light up and when it did we would place more coal lumps on top of all this, and then place an open newspaper sheet over the fire opening which "drew" the air above form the chimney opening. You tried to time it that when you saw a brown stain appearing on the newspaper sheet you would draw it quickly away as the fire had caught light. Although sometimes you weren't quick enough and the sheet of newspaper caught fire and with a great big "Whump" the lit sheet of newspaper flew up the lum but you had succeeded in lighting the coal fire.

Only thing I didn't like about lighting the coal fire was in the morning time when you got up, you had to empty last night's ashes from the grate and put them in a couple of sheets of newspaper, wrap them all up like a parcel and dump them in the back court midden. I'm sure that like me some were given this job on your way to school, I learned to stand well back from the midden when I threw the ashes [wrapped in newspaper] into it as one time a rat jumped out at me and scared the bloomin life out of me.

Nowadays of course we have central heating throughout our houses so the art form of lighting the fire is almost a thing of the past but we remember don't we. Lol.

Where did we go.

With the regeneration of the Gorbals area we knew that Oatlands would follow suit, which was such a shame, there was a refurbishment plan tried out in the red sandstone tenements but was deemed a failure and although the open spaces lay for years eventually the regeneration of Oatlands did happen. Of course this meant a great displacement of people everywhere.

Some moved to the Gorbals , others to different areas of Glasgow or many others moved to the housing schemes and some even moved overseas to other countries but what we will never forget wherever we went to, was that growing up in Oatlands was such a wonderful happy time or God's little acre as it was often called. I have to say that those were my happiest days when the summers always seemed to be so hot and the winter times so very cold and nothing better if it was that cold that the ducksy over at Richmond park froze over and all us weans were sliding on the ice and even some weans had ice skates but for me it was just sliding along the ice, nowadays I have to use a walking stick to get about but when I see snow falling here in London it still makes me smile to see my grandweans enjoying themselves and think oh wouldn't it be great to be a wean again. This is me with my thoughts as I say in London, while many other Oatlands people moved farther away to Canada/U.S.A, Spain , South Africa etc, or perhaps maybe another part of Glasgow, but wherever we went we will never forget our formative years in Oatlands will we. !! Such a great childhood we all experienced and when I see weans of today playing with their computers and video games, I actually feel sorry that they will never share the experiences we all had growing up as weans in Oatlands playing outside from morning till night [school holidays]

Chapter 10

Polmadie rd [east side] to Queensferry st.

Polmadie rd [east side] to Queensferry St.

Now let us take a walk up Polmadie rd from the bottom of Rutherglen rd, first of all we have the Piccadilly cafe where they sold beautiful ice-cream with raspberry sauce over it that you would die for. It was owned by the Tartaglia family and it was here where a lot of boys and girls met up to have a coca cola and listen to the pop records on the juke box and talk teenage talk.

Billy Scorgie's family lived in number 3 Polmadie rd.

Then as we move along we had a launderette and I believe [a wet fish shop??] then Cochranes shop on the corner as we came to Rosebery st.

On the point of Rosebery st can you remember when the man with the pony and trap came he would charge the weans a penny to sit in the trap which held about twenty weans and he would drive them along to Granton st and then back to Rosebery st at Polmadie rd again. All the weans would be shouting and waving at people as they were drove along the street pure magic.

Then crossing over going up Polmadie rd we came to a hairdressers shop between Rosebery st and Cramond st, I can still see all those lovely red sandstone tenement buildings standing there when I close my eyes, what a shame they were demolished. Then between Cramond st and Toryglen st we had Milfred Moores bakers shop [but this shop wasn't opened to the public as it was in here he done his baking].

On the corner of Toryglen st we had a petrol station where the black hackney taxi's went at tea break, then you had Scott's beef factory behind and the Gypsey's place, also there was a Mrs Brown who lived on the same landing as my Granny Hendry in Wolseley st who had a wee chicken coop there, I remember this because one day I was passing by there and Mrs Brown called me over and gave me two newly laid eggs and I couldn't rush home quick enough to give them to my Ma.

After this going up Polmadie rd we came to the Caledonia brick works where there were thousands of bricks laying about in big heaps just waiting to be loaded up into lorries and taken to building sites throughout Glasgow I remember one day when I was at Big Bonnies school a class mate of mine said lets go and play in the brick yard on Polmadie rd, we did and when dinner time was over and we should have gone back to school we never. We plunked school for the half day and we were climbing over all these bricks having a great time. I thought I was clever because I went back to Fauldhouse st and when big Bonnies school came out I walked up our stairs and into my house but what a telling aff I got from my Ma, When I hadn't shown up in class in the afternoon, my big sister Jeanette who also attended big Bonnies was called for to see if was ill. She told my Ma as soon as she got in from school and I was found out. I wasn't allowed out of the house after school had finished for the rest of the week and could only watch my wee pals playing football in the street. That learned me a lesson , no more plunking school. Lol.

These brick kilns were obviously very hot to bake the clay and make them into bricks and a lot of night times [especially in the winter months] some men who had fallen on hard times and had nowhere to sleep, would sleep inside the brick factory beside the kilns for heat.

Some of these men would come round our back courts and sing to try and get a few pennies for food and I always remember my Ma would throw a few coins down to them in the back court when they came round singing and she said to me son you never know what has happened to that man in his life and it's true, as the old saying goes, "there but for the grace of God go I."

There was a freightliner depot called Ferry Master later on and this was just before Polmadie Locomotive engine sheds which I have talked about before. Opposite the sheds was where the British Oxygen Company had a big plant, this plant had a few fire scares over the years and what a disaster it would have been if there had been an explosion!!

On Polmadie rd and further up a fair bit you then had Hampden park the national stadium and when there was an international football match or a cup final being played then Polmadie rd was absolutely packed with fans walking up it and remember there was another great wee football team called Third Lanark [Hi Hi] just beside Holyrood school and they always got a good attendance but unfortunately they went into liquidation years ago. I remember that years ago they had a great wee goalkeeper called Jocky Robertson and Dave Hilly and a few other players but sadly they folded up.

Toryglen st

Now coming back down Polmadie rd we arrive back at Toryglen st and we take a walk along it and come to Rosebery park which was the home of Shawfield juniors that Frank Mclintock, Davie Holt etc played for. It was a fair sized pitch and people who were living in the tenements who lived up on the top floor would get seeing a free match from their windows when they were all playing. Sadly over the years this park closed down too with health hazard warnings placed outside its perimeter wall.

Then going past Rosebery park we came to Dalmeny st/Granton st/Rosyth st which were nicknamed the "grey square" these were another lot of "new houses" that were built in between the two wars 1920/30's . Still staying on Toryglen st we came to Rosyth rd at the bottom which never had any houses built on it but was more or less an entrance to the industrial estate that had many different units in it.

There were quite a few and over the years some were replaced with others, you had Landers alarms, Craig Nicol, Mr Gaughan's yard, the Gypseys, timber yard, Collins textiles, Polmadie training workshop, a Territorial army base [for a while] SCS industrial cleaners, and heavy goods vehicles yard. In fact it was quite a big area and my school class friend Geana Mcpike [Sweeney] had her first job when she left school with Craig Nicol there aged fifteen.

Rosyth st./Granton st.

Coming back down Rosyth rd we carry on with Rosyth st where the Howitt family lived at number 1 and I also remember two of my school class pals Peter Donachie and Bobby Doran lived here I remember when we had the eleven plus exam in Wee Bonnies Peter passed with top marks but refused to go to Holyrood senior secondary school as a few of his cousins and pals were at Big Bonnies Junior secondary school, and with Peter refusing to go to Holyrood he went on to attend Big Bonnies school and was in the same class as me there. Also in Rosyth st we had Gary Taylor who lived at number 11 and Anne Marie McKee who lived at number 12. We turned left at the bottom of Rosyth st and into Roseberry st and again turn left into Granton st where James "Jamie" McKenzie had moved to from 135 Rosebery st, also Michelle Findlay lived here at number 12 Granton st. Then we move along Granton st to the top and turn right into Toryglen st, go along a wee bit and turn right again into Dalmeny st, on the other side you had the tenements and Dalmeny st lead right through to Rutherglen rd.

I have to say that because I lived in Fauldhouse st which was a fair bit away I wasn't down this end of Oatlands too often but when I did then I always remember the people out in their gardens of the "new houses" and there were always plenty of weans playing in the front gardens and plenty of laughter, it was the laughter and happiness that stuck in my mind but not only the "new houses" but in the low doon windows of the tenements there was always a gathering of people exchanging news [oh and a wee bit of gossip].

That is the abiding memory that I will always have of Oatlands, the peoples cheerfulness and close knit spirit.

101 trolley bus.

So now take a wee walk back towards Queensferry st and do you remember the old 101 trolley buses that terminated there and you and your pals would always try and "cadge a hudgie" when the 101 left its terminus but the conductor knew what we were up to ha ha. As the 101 made its way along Rosebery st we passed by Billy Moore's dairy shop in the tenements and further along just before turning into Dalmeny st we had a wee newsagents shop owned by a George Robertson in 107 Roseberry st, he also had another newsagents just round the corner in Rutherglen rd.

Dalmeny st.

Dalmeny st is where a friend of mine Christina Milarvie Quarrel dwelt and she lived top floor at number 60 in a single end, she had a wonderful T shirt printed about Dalmeny st with 3 weans photo printed on the back of it and I have inserted it among my photos in this book for you all to have a look at.

Dalmeny st had a few shops in it like Mr Singhs shop [a guy who lived next door to Mr Singhs used to make football rattles for people] which was at the top end of Dalmeny st near to Toryglen st. Colin Mackie tells me that when he was a wean his Mother [Myra] used to send him with a "tick note" as did lots of families back then to get messages on the "tick" until payday on Friday, and Colin would "add" on in his own handwriting a few things like ginger and sweeties but Mr Singh wasn't daft and sussed the different handwriting out. Of course at the Rutherglen rd end of Dalmeny st who could forget Jimmy's cafe at the corner of Dalmeny st/Rutherglen rd, Jimmy had a candy floss machine and orange juice machine etc and loads of sweeties too and Angela Burns who had a Saturday job there said she often lost her Saturday jobs wages playing his one armed bandit!! Eddie and May's off license shop faced opposite Jimmy's cafe on the other corner of Dalmeny st.

Then there was Marion's dairy in Dalmeny st with Jeanette Queen working behind the counter.

Dalmenny st also had a public phone box in it [or were there two?] as I said before back in the 1950's and even 60's most people never had a landline phone in their houses.

Cramond st.

So now we come to Cramond st that ran from Dalmeny st through to Polmadie rd and where Colin Mackie, his mother and father Myra and David and his siblings Jeanette and wee Davie [R.I.P] lived happily, although Colin would move quite a few times to other addresses in Oatlands. While Colin was living here at number 74 Cramond st the family that lived directly above him was Martin and Betty Curran and their weans, Martin lived here for nine years, leaving in 1970 out to East Kilbride where he still lives today, sadly his lovely wife Betty has passed away. God watch over her.

Milfred Moore had one of his bakers shops here in Cramond st and can you remember those lovely rolls with stewed sausages and onions oh la la.

Angela Gillies lived in Cramond st and gave a voice recording in Oatlands Memories Facebook page run by Colin Mackie of her time living there.I believe there were two Dairy shops in Cramond st, one was Bryce's dairy and the other was Betty Knoxs dairy.

Now leaving Cramond st behind us we walk down Polmadie rd [again] and turn right into Rosebery st and again more of those lovely red sandstone tenement buildings. It really breaks my heart when I think of how these grand buildings are no longer with us.

May Sweeney Bishop also lived in 15 Cramond st. When she married [?]

Rosebery st

Who can ever forget Wullie Scorgie's newsagent shop ran by him and his wife Isa [not forgetting "Shelia" the wire haired fox terrier dog] and that lovely homemade tablet that he made. Wullie was also a prolific writer of poems and his son Billy has kindly sent me one of his Da's poems which I have shown in my Miscellaneous chapter which is chapter 11. Danny Sweeney and Frank McLintock were both paperboys for Wullie.

Tam Leonard [who tended to lots of the gardens in the "new houses" in Oatlands] had a sister called Cathy and she moved from the Gorbals to Rosebery st after her Ma had moved there. Jean Shreenan told me that she herself lived in 52 Roseberry st and Tam and his Ma lived on the same landing as her. All of the women used to congregate outside of Cathy's low doon window every day waiting on the weans coming out of school, May Miller's Ma who was one of the crowd and she was a comedian, she had everybody in stitches every day in Rosebery st. Cathy lived on the opposite side of the street from Jean Shreenan.

Also in Rosebery st you had Cochrane's shop on the corner of Rosebery st/Polmadie rd then Wullie Scorgies newsagents, Sally Feeley's fruit shop, Tommy + Mary Parker-Holme's bakers shop and finally just before Dalmeny st you had Hollands dairy [some people called it Mulhollands !!] all these shops were on the same side of Roseberry st with Willie Leslie's butchers shop being on the opposite side of the street, after his death his two sons Jimmy and Charlie ran the shop.

Rutherglen rd shops.

We now take a walk along Rutherglen rd and we start with the shops there at the start we had the Piccadilly cafe, Louie the barbers shop,the Transport cafe, Walkers the opticians, a fishmongers shop, Peggy the drapers shop, and Sadie's fruit shop and then Jimmy's cafe. This has us arriving at Dalmeny st and we cross over and continue walking along Rutherglen rd and we have Eddie and May's off license shop, a shop selling cold meats then no more shops till we came to Tommy Robertson's newsagents and then the Wee Mill /Chancers pub and this takes us to Queensferry st. [At a later date we had Sol's shop, a bookies and Jimmy's cafe became a hairdressers shop and Eddies off license was taken over by a man called Paul]. It was here at Queensferry st we had the 101 trolley bus terminus and Jenny's burn. I know as I write my book that just over in Richmond park there is a new pub/Restaurant and it is called Jenny Burn.

Chancers/Wee Mill pub.

Was ran by a lady called Mary in the late 70's early 80's, Martin Sweeney was the manager for a while when Chancers took over from the Wee Mill. Jim Woods ran Chancers bar with his wife Heather and son Jim Jnr., it was a great wee pub. He always took the people away on bus runs - Blackpool - Leven - Rothesay, Jim owned the pub and had so many regular customers in his time there, one being Rab Hay who drank in there when it started off as Chancers and he was a regular in there all the way through until it closed.

Joe McBride's daughter Julie managed the wee Mill before it changed to Chancers, Betty Miller ran quiz nights, Bingo and also had a DJ on Saturday nights, on Monday nights they had the dominoes teams, Tuesday pub dominoes, Thursday night quiz night and Friday night was Bingo night. Such a shame we don't have pubs like that in Oatlands anymore Eh!!

Author's summing up of chapter 10:

Well we have taken a walk up Polmadie rd starting off at the Piccadilly cafe and walking past the few shops that were there, past Cramond st and Toryglen st, past the petrol station, Caledonia brick making yard and up to Polmadie locomotive engine sheds. Over the bridge where people walked every day going either to Calder st and Holyrood schools [in all sorts of weather] passing the "Clenny" department Malls Mire and up to Hampden park and Cathkin park where Third Lanark played.

Then along Toryglen st where the singer/showman Glen Daly, Bill Hands, Mr Japp my old PT teacher from Big Bonnies school and many many others lived over the years.

Rosebery park which was named after the former prime minister the 5th earl of Rosebery, where Shawfield juniors once played 1918-1960 [Pollock FC 1926-28]. Following the demise of Shawfield juniors. Glasgow corporation education committee arranged to buy the ground in 1961 for school football competitions. Sadly later it closed down because it was found to be contaminated by chrome waste from factories in nearby Shawfield and had warning signs posted to keep the public out. James "Jamie" McKenkie said to me you know we used to play in the "jelly mallow" and we never realised playing in those craters what a danger it was. Of course we also visited all the factories beside and next to Rosebery park and to be truthful there were quite a few over the years giving employment to many Oatlands people.

Then we took a walk down to where the "grey square" buildngs were in Rosyth/ Granton /Dalmeny streets which were always referred to as "the new houses" and even though they were built between 1920/30's they were still called the "new houses" in the 60's/ 70's and 80's etc it like a lot of things it gets a nickname and it sticks over the years.

We took a trip along Rosebery st where memories of the old 101 trolley bus which used to run along there is still fresh in my mind, I'm taking about all of the 1950's here and right up to December 1960 when my tenement collapsed and we were moved to south Nitshill but even as a 70 year old man writing this book those memories are still as fresh as they were back then. I have a friend Alexis Rutherford who lived in Rosebery st but later on she moved to the Gorbals where she lives now, there always was a great interchange of people flitting to the Gorbals from Oatlands and vice-versa over the years. Then we took in Dalmeny st with Jimmy's cafe and Mr Singhs shop to mention just a few before going along Cramond st and Milford Moores shop which sold those lovely rolls, then off we went along Rutherglen rd past the Piccadilly cafe heading along to Queensferry st and Chancers pub and Jenny's burn where if you remember in the summer time it could "smell to the high Heavens", you looked at Jenny's burn and all the different colours of yellow and green in it, caused by Whites chemical factory emptying its waste into it. No wonder you never saw anyone fishing in Jenny's burn!!

Now this just leaves the last part of Richmond park opposite Rutherglen rd and what can we say that hasn't been said before about the "Richy" although at this section of the park we had its two best known parts, yes the swing park and the "ducksy". I always remember using the monkey ladder where you tried to swing from rung to rung but halfway through most of us got sore arms and dropped down [with our arms having grown another couple of inches. Lol.] Not forgetting that big "chute" where you placed grease proof bread wrapper under your "bahooky" to make you go faster and the funny thing is it seemed to work!!

Yes the "ducksy" what memories do we all hold of it, feeding the swans, hiring one of those "pedlo boats", playing a game of putting, watching the "old men" sitting down at the boathouse and playing a game of chess, moving the chess pieces with long poles with a wire attached to the end of it. Then also thinking back to when the pond froze over in the Winter times and it seemed as if every wean from Oatlands was trying out their skating skills.

I have posted a photo of the "ducksy" frozen over [photo taken by James Currie a relation of Colin Mackie's] and weans skating on it.

Overall Richmond park was a wonderful place for us weans to play in and for our parents to take a stroll with the family. I know it has changed over the years with houses being built on it. I don't agree with this at all but it has happened and so we have to make the most of what we have left of the original Richmond park. Most people, especially of my generation will remember it the way it was back in those days of the 1950's/ 60's/70's.

One event that does stick in my mind was on Ester Sunday morning my Ma would make hard boiled eggs for my sister and me and we would paint wee faces on them, then roll them down one of the wee braes in Richmond park, chase after them and when we got to them we would crack the shells open and eat them. This was to commemorate Easter time and the boulders being removed outside the cave that Our Lord emerged from.

Chapter 11

More Peoples stories

David Leishman.

I was born at 24 Mathieson st in 1949 across from the side entrance to St Francis's in a front door house, basically a single end and I lived there until I was about 5 years old.

Being so young one of the things that always stuck in my mind was the rat catcher putting the traps under the floor tae catch the long tails, the houses were old and in disrepair, we then moved to Oatlands to 11 Cramond st where I grew up. Oatlands has many memories for me, we used to play up in the brickwork in Polmadie rd and we had a great time up there. There was also a wee puggy train that would collect the clay from the Malls Mire and bring it down to the brickwork to be processed into bricks. I also remember the old dossers who would sleep up there as it was warm from the kilns. It was a hard life for those poor souls.

I was always up to some mischief as young boys did back in those days, hudgies on the back of the midgie motors going up tae the Clenny in Polmadie. I worked for a man called Davy Kinghorn, he had a horse and cart delivering milk, eggs and butter, this meant that I had to get up early in the mornings. Then after that it was off to school but some days we would "plunk" school and go up to the Malls Mire to play where Whites chemical works were. It was from there that a lot of the pollution that went intae Jenny's burn came from and then flowed intae the river Clyde, nae health and safety then.

I left Wolseley st school and went to Calder st secondary school, I didnae like school and was always getting the belt but when I look back a good boot up the backside is what I needed.

As a teenager we would go into the Piccadilly cafe which was at the corner of Polmadie rd and Rutherglen rd. That was the in place if you had any money and I always had ways of earning a few bob. We would break up sticks and sell them round the doors. We would also go up tae the railway at Polmadie at night to get coal and sell that too.

We had plenty of customers and we kept a lot of houses warm in those days. Wee rogues we were but that was life in those days.

Another thing that will stay with me always was a trip tae the pawn in Braehead st on Monday after school, Dad's suit or auld Maw's wedding ring "whisper your name so naebody can hear you"!! Many a dinner was put on the table fae Uncle John's the pawn but time moves on.

We started having oor first pints of beer and Hurrel's would be our first pub back then, the rest of the pubs widnae serve us as we were too young. I remember there were plenty of pubs back in Oatlands then. My local years later was the Splash bar on Polmadie rd, and my older brother's local was the Malls Mire also on Polmadie rd. There were real characters in those days, best not to mention any names so nobody gets intae trouble that way, aye, there was plenty of ducking and diving around those two pubs then.

Anyway time moves on and Oatlands by this time was getting a bit run doon, I got married and still stayed in Oatlands and that's the time when they started pulling part of it down to renovate the buildings. It wisnae the same place after that so it was time to move on. We went to Castlemilk and I hated the place but we had a young family then, now they're all grown up and doing well for themselves.

I'm divorced and now live in Lochwinnoch and I love it, I retired and a few years ago got a wee car so I'm off out most days and make the most of it.

Life is too short, so enjoy yourself, that's my motto.

Karen Doherty [Laverty]

We are the Laverty family all born in at 196 Wolseley st, Oatlands, Glasgow. There are six of us, three girls Margo, Karen [me] and Renee [Catherine] who is the eldest and then three boys, Brian. Austin and Pauric. I was born in June 1960, my Mother and Father were from Donegal in Ireland and they left there to come to Glasgow to work.

My Father worked as a builders labourer on different building sites and then later in the tunnels while my Mother worked as a clippie on Glasgow buses. They were introduced to each other in Glasgow and later got married in St Francis's Chapel, Cumberland st Gorbals.

I have only great memories of growing up in Oatlands. We all attended "Wee Bonnies" and the school teachers that I remember were Miss Marshall, she was the nicest, kindest teacher you could ask for. There was also a Miss McConnell and a Mr Feeley. I went to school there until 1971 and then went to Craigie st secondary school until 1973 which is when we went to live in Donegal. I was thirteen years old then and couldn't wait to get there as we had been there on holiday the previous year or two. We holidayed at my Granny Laverty's [my Da's Mother] in a small town called Stranorlar. The holidays there were great as we were allowed so much more freedom and getting to run through fields and streams was something new to us all and although the town was only small it was only a five minute walk to the local shops.

We were brought up in the tenements in Oatlands in a "single end" as they were called, I can still see the layout of the house very clearly in my mind. There was a living room/kitchen and this room had a recess where my Mother and Father had their bed, then there were was an open fireplace and an electric cooker. The sink was under the window looking down to the "back courts" where we often played and the "midgie bins" were out there. We used to climb the dykes and then jump off them onto a pile of old mattresses that we had laid on the ground below us. There could have been 10 or 20 of us at any one time and you had to prove how brave you were by jumping. We also "dreeped" down the walls and dykes. We often laughed about how children were washed standing up in the kitchen sink on a Saturday night and we would sit on top of the dykes pointing and laughing at someone getting bathed and when the child would see us pointing and heard us laughing at them they would try and cover themselves up, only to get a slap from their Mammy who told them to stand up as she hadn't seen us laughing at her child.

The people who lived beside us and who we played with were the O'Donnell's who were all girls, Moira, Eileen, Brenda and later on Ann. Other people's names were the Melly's, who were John, Carmel, Michael and Celine and they all moved over to Donegal a few years before we did. I have met up with four of them since and when I did they told me what a wee "red headed devil" I was. There were also the Comiskys, Henry and Dominic, then the Brogan's Tommy, Margaret and Hughie. Another family were the Walkers, Glynn and Yvonne who were twins form Elmfoot st. The Brogan's moved from Wolseley st to Logan st, but I'm not sure where the Comiskys went to.

Another place we would have spent a lot of time in was "Henny's scrap metal shop", he lived down on the ground floor [or low doon as we used to call it] and out the back and was very good to us all. My brother Austin was forever "nicking" copper and lead and taking it into Henny's for money. Times were tough then and our Mammy was glad of a few extra bob. Henny gave me my first transistor radio which was never turned off.

Richmond park was another playground for us and the sand pit [sonny pon] through to the duck pond [ducksie] where the poor "parkie" must have been demented by us as were always trying to get a "free go" on the paddle boats. My youngest brother fell in one day and he was pure green with slime and gunge and absolutely stinking when we pulled him out, he was only about 4 years old at the time.

Another thing that sticks in my mind is when a couple of old cars were found in a lock up in the pen[d] which ran through between Polmadie rd and Elmfoot st. These cars were found because my brother Austin and a cousin got this lock up and found a load of old newspapers which they tried to sell to people in the street. One man came over to buy one and realised that the papers were years old. I think they were dated pre-war bur were in very good condition, the boys were asked where they got them from and the police were called in. The police then asked them where they got them from and they had to show them where. There was a lot of excitement going on and lot of people gathered in the street to see what was going on. The fire brigade were called in too and as they brought the old cars out they were covered in muck and stinking, so the fire brigade hosed them down as they came out of the lock up. I clearly remember the shiny red leather seats and the cars looked to be in great condition for pre-war cars. This happened I think in 1969 and as far as I heard they were taken to a transport museum.

Our house was "one up" and our bedroom looked into the street, there were two double beds, one for the three boys and one for us three girls. There were many a pillow fight in that room and once we broke the bed frame of the boys bed as we were all bouncing on it and nearly went through to the floor below. The wee man who lived below us was knocking on up on his ceiling with a brush. There was a good long hallway from our room to the kitchen and the hallway had another door and this is where the coal bunker was kept for our open fire. We had no inside toilet, just a bucket for during the night otherwise we would have had to walk down to the stair head toilet on our half landing below.

My poor Mammy must have been nearly demented by us, our Dad worked away during the week so it wasn't easy for her on her own with six of us and at least three of us being complete tearaways. Daddy would always bring a load of sweeties on a Friday night when he came home and waken us up, it was like a party every Friday night. We were seldom in the house during the day after school and during the school summer holidays, if we were hungry we would stand in the back court and call up to Mammy for a "piece on jam" or sugar. It would be wrapped up in bread paper and thrown out of the window to you below and everyday was like having a picnic.

Every evening we gathered in Elmfoot st to play games such as kick the can, animals, Chinese ropes and balls or football. We had jumble sales on the pavements where we could sell old toys and clothes or anything we could gather up and sometimes we made a few bob at them. Weddings were another way of making money and we went mainly up Polmadie rd on Saturdays for "the scramble" after the wedding service. There was many a skint knee in the battle to see who could get to the money first as it was thrown from the wedding car as it drove off. I loved it and we always took the money we got back home to Mammy and she would give us some back to go to wee Jeannie McCann's shop or another shop on Polmadie rd. We'd always ask for the "penny tray" and browse for ages to pick up what we wanted. There was also a bakery on Rutherglen rd and we went there and asked for a penny's worth of broken biscuits.

Another memory was getting away on school trips from "Wee Bonnies". Once when we went to Millport and the coach took us to the ferry and we had all been given a packed lunch but told not to eat it before we got there but most of us had it scoffed on the bus, then the poor teacher would be running around with sick bags to us all. We hired bikes out once we got to Millport and also played on the "crocodile rock".

Before we left to go to live in Donegal a lot of houses in front of Wolseley st and surrounding areas had become derelict and there was massive "spare grun" and and it was here we built "huts" using old doors and linoleum taken from these empty houses. The doors were stacked in a square shape and we put the lino over the top of them and added more doors on top of this and it gave us a two story house and we filled it with old furniture that people had left behind when they moved. We had a great time building houses and we would also see who could smash the most windows of these derelict houses, what a brilliant pastime. And we had a pile of stones at the ready. The police came but never tried to stop us as the houses were going to be demolished anyway.

We left on Guy Fawkes night 1973, a mini bus took us, our cases and small items of furniture, we were all sick on the boat, a bit like a Billy Connolly moment throw up, then run and explore the boat ha ha.

Arriving in Ireland, passing through Northern Ireland where "the troubles" were in full swing, there were soldiers everywhere. We were stopped a few times and the soldiers spoke to us and my wee brothers were excited to see real guns for the first time and asked the "sodjers" for a go!! We all knew the answer to that question but the soldiers were nice and asked us where we were going to live.

Arriving in Donegal we drove down a different road from where we had went to on holidays. It was a long quiet road with no cars on it. We pulled into the street of a farmyard with a very big house, here we were met by my aunties Molly and Pauline both sisters of my Mother. They had a fire lit in the range in the kitchen we had never seen a range before and you could cook on top of it.

I got a black eye within minutes of getting off the bus, in our excitement we couldn't wait to see around this big house and as I ran through the hallway to go upstairs to see the four bedrooms I turned to catch the banister but I fell and hit my eye on the stairs, so I had a black eye within seconds. "welcome to your new home." Hah! My aunties had polished the floors so well they were like ice rinks.

We had four bedrooms upstairs and one bedroom, a sitting room and a scullery downstairs. So you can imagine the difference that was from a single end slap bang in the middle of Oatlands to a big house with no shops or anything else within two miles, except for the cows and fields.

There was an orchard at the bottom of the garden which had apples, pears and plums growing in it and the river was just through a fence there too. There were a couple of byres and a hen house and Mammy got a few hens. We had great fun with them after we lost the fear of them. The hen house had twenty one nests in it, they went all the way around and each nest had a wee door that had a chain attached to it. The chain was for sliding the hatch/door of the nest up and we were sent out in the morning to let the hens out. My sister Renee [Catherine] and myself were usually sent and we would pull the hatch up and wait till the hen put its head out and then drop the hatch again, kind of trapping the hen. I'm sitting here having a laugh thinking back on this as the hens would be squawking so much my Mother thought they were laying. Needless to say few eggs were laid by those hens [I wonder why!]. We also had a cow and a calf, we were scared of the cow too but soon got used to it and fed her biscuits.

I dreaded the thought of going to school here and fought the bit out about going, I was told if I got a job then I wouldn't have to go to school, so me and my older sister Margo [she was 14 and I was 13] walked the two miles to get the bus which would take us to Letterkenny which was our nearest town. We tried cafes, shops and supermarkets with no luck, so we went another day and tried the factories. There was a sweet factory called Oatfields, they made Emerald sweeties amongst others, but were mostly known for Emeralds. We had no luck there so we tried another factory called Gaeltex, this factory made dresses and aprons. We lied about our ages I said I was 15 and my sister said she was 16. We got started in there and learned how to use a sewing machine. My sister loved it and was great at it but to be honest all I did was to carry on with all the others who worked there, I certainly never earned a week's wages in there. We earned £7.50pence a week while we were being trained, so as far as I was concerned I could work my socks off or do very little and still get the same money, so I did very little. I was there for about 18 months and was taken to the office every Friday for many weeks and threatened with the sack. The boss was a Scotsman called Bill Orr and I don't know why he kept me on as long as he did, maybe because I was a cheeky Glasgow girl. I just enjoyed going in for the carry on and on a Friday night we all went to the dance in Letterkenny at the Fiesta ballroom. There were live bands every week and it was always packed, it was always good fun.

After living in the house that we first came to for about a year and a half we moved to a place called "Corkey", there was one long row of houses but it was great for us because we were back to street lighting and having people around of our own age to mix with. It was always pitch black at the first house we lived because it was so far out on its own although we were now near plenty of other houses, we still had no running water so we had to go to the well to fetch buckets of water at least two or three times a day. The well had a running tap on it and there was always a water fight at it as everyone kind of went for the water around the same time every evening, we had some great times living there and taught the neighbours some of the games we played back in Oatlands.

We are all still living here in Ireland except for one brother who lives and works in London. My eldest sister has been back in Glasgow a few times since we left and I have been to Ayr a few times and Glasgow twice. The last time was about 12 years ago and there were such big changes, all the houses we lived in were gone but there was still Wolseley st. I was able to walk from Queens park to Richmond park and my old street and all around the area. It was good to go back but sad to see all the changes in the area.

My brother was over in Glasgow for a few days just a couple of months ago [April 2017] he couldn't find places he remembered but he was in Glasgow green and remembered there. I have a hankering to go over again soon and see the changes. My brother has suggested we all go over together and see what we think, so hopefully we will.

All I can honestly say is, it was a brilliant place to spend your childhood and memories last forever, so Glasgow and especially Oatlands will always have a special place in my heart.

Linda Stephenson [Orr]

I was born at 29 Logan st Oatlands, Glasgow. My Mammy and Daddy were Ellen [Nellie] and John Bing. I had an older sister Helen and we both attended Wolseley st school in 1960 and after that went onto Adelphi Comprehensive.

Our back garden was Richmond park where Dad played bowls and took us over for a game of putting and over to the "ducksy" to feed the ducks followed by a "pokey hat" ice cream. We then moved around to the veranda houses and ours was 30 Elmfoot st and we spent the rest of our childhood there before they started pulling all the buildings down.

Everything was dark and bleak, a vibrant wee place was bulldozed. I lost friends from school as they moved out to Castlemilk a housing scheme in Glasgow. It was a BIG void in my young life, I have a lot of happy memories, though, but the clearances were wrong and it's heartbreaking to see Richmond park slowly being taken away.

I got married in 1972 then I moved to Govanhill and then later Rutherglen.

I have a brick from where I lived at 29 Logan st and an "Oatlands" plaque at my door, my daughter bought me a lovely painting of an old Tram with "Oatlands" on its destination board. My sister still lives there in the new builds and like myself she is a proud Oatlander. Two people that I would love to mention are Betty Hobbins and Robert Cameron, he lived and worked there all of his life.

I get very nostalgic when I go back and have mixed emotions.

Author's note:

The Betty Hobbins that Linda is talking about lived at 176 Wolseley st on the same landing as Jean Shreenan, Betty planted a tree in their front garden of their "new hoose" and it really flourished it was always admired by everyone.

Neil Macowan.

I was born in the hospital annexed to Lennox castle, which was used as a maternity hospital for some time in the 1950's which means I can technically say I was born in a castle.

At that time the family lived in Cramond st, Oatlands. The singer Donovan lived nearby and my Mum used to babysit for him when he was a wean.

The family then moved to Kerrycroy street in Toryglen, a new housing scheme in those days and I remember my Nana describing the new flats as being "like paradise" compared to the old house. Making new friends was no problem and I think going to Toryglen primary school was my first school. My memories of that time included playing "doorbell skoosh" around the area, I also went to the "wedding scrambles" and going over the Malls Mire when the football was on at Hampden park to collect the empty "gingies" and beer bottles off of the supporters buses that parked there.

When I was seven or eight years old my Mother remarried and we moved up the west end of Glasgow, I didn't have much problem fitting in there either although I made friends with a "problematic" boy who had been expelled from his previous school and we remained pals right up to the 80's which is when I lost track of him.

Nowadays I live in Spain and usually go back at Christmas time to Glasgow/Scotland to visit friends and family, I'm always surprised by how much the old place has changed. Everything is gentrified now and lots of things are either gone or changed beyond recognition but it's still the dear green place.

Linda McGovern.

The Lowe Family.

I have wonderful memories of old Oatlands before the decanting and shoddy refurbishment. There were 4 of us, my brother James, my youngest brother Derek and my sister Agnes.

The house [we called it a house] was a room and kitchen with outside toilet and no hot water. This was 19 Rosebery street and this had been my Grandfathers house where he had brought up 5 of a family, one of them being my Mother, so she was a real "oatcake from Oatlands"

Our close was between Wullie Scorgies and Mrs Feeleys fruit shop, a wee bit further on was Parkers the dairy and at the top of the street was Mullhollands dairy [some say it was actually called Hollands instead of Mullholland], facing us was Leslie the butchers with the best square sausage going.

On a good summers day my Da would lean out of the windae as we were low down and caw the rope for me and my sister Angela the other end of the rope tied to the lamppost.

Wullie Scorgies was where that the "Christmas club" was joined and I remember buying my mum 2 black cats for the fireplace by saving my penny every Saturday. In the summer Mr Scorgie would come out with his brown coat on and pullover the canopy and then you knew it was summer and it was Walls ice cream time.

Mrs Feeley fruit shop had sacks of potatoes and Mrs Feeley would put on her rubber gloves to weigh you out 3 lb of potatoes. My Mum [Ma] would arrange for us four to get an apple and crisps for our dinner all through the summer holidays, and they would get paid on a Friday from Mrs Feeley then it was off to Richmond park with our picnic.

Rutherglen rd was packed with shops, Miss Winks was the boutique, Frames for the roller blinds for the windows and the treat on a

Saturday was "the Oddspot restaurant" which was actually a cafe for mince and tatties, a new pair of shoes could be bought from Greendales footwear shop.

Facing the shops on Rutherglen rd was the Richmond park which housed the "ducksy", the sandy park with the swing park and the shows at the Glasgow fair, oh the lovely memories now when you look back.

On Polmadie rd there was St Margaret, right next to a row of shops. There was Curries the newsagents then McCanns shop that sold everything from nylons to nails. The Splash pub and of course Mario's the chippy which was always packed on a Friday night. We always got a chippy tea as Friday was the "the steamie" night everything stripped, bedcovers, curtains the lot. Saturday morning was hot bath and a towel for the folk that had no bath or inside toilet but 50% of Oatlands had no bath or inside toilet unless you lived in the pre-war houses which included Rosyth st and Granton st.

When I was eleven years old we moved from Rosebery st up to the posher part of Oatlands, across the way was Shawfield stadium which was packed on a Friday night, then of course across the road we had the "Jenny's burn" which had dirty coloured water running into it from Whites chemical factory but all the colours looked wonderful to us weans.

Childhood memories of a place called Oatlands that will always conjure up love in my heart.

Author's note:

People will all remember when Shawfield stadium was packed on Friday nights because of the greyhound racing held there, most men were paid on a Friday night back then and made a bee line to back the races but a lot of the guys after working hard all week lost most of their wages and had to go back and face the wife. I'm not saying all men but some of them who had a gambling habit.

Chapter 12

Miscellaneous

Oatlands Memories.

I have to give many thanks to our own Colin Mackie for starting up the Oatlands Memories Facebook site where we all post and answer comments about Oatlands. We also have a large selection of photos sent in by people over the years and if anyone reading my book hasn't paid a visit to it then please do, you never know you may see an old photo of yourself there. I know my primary school photo is on show from Wee Bonnies and others from Wolseley st school, too.

There is also an added extra that gives us a chance to listen to Oatlands people speaking of their memories of living in Oatlands when you click onto the home page, there are a lot of topics you can click onto like "the steamie" where once again people have written down their experiences or even listen to yours truly singing my version of "China doll" or trying to sing that should be. lol.

There's also a topic about Polmadie bridge and what is happening to it, and people "down our street" again giving their own account of what it was like to live in Oatlands before the regeneration happened and people speaking about "the Richy."

Of course we have several videos showing the old buildings, one where Billy Connolly sings a sad lament through it and also one of Irishman Tony Kelly telling us about Rosyth st where he used to live and about his good friend Cathy, every time I watch this wee video it makes me very nostalgic indeed and at the end of it Tony says but "where did everybody go". The answer to that is we went everywhere, other parts of Glasgow and indeed other countries.

So a big thanks to you once again Colin for giving us Oatlands Memories Facebook site. We really all do appreciate your hard work.

Isolated Oatlands

The queerest place in all the world
this without a doubt
For when a man comes here to stay
he simply can't get out
He'll never see Auld Brigton for the
Brig's now almost down
An' there's not a single car or a bus
to take him to the Town.

Hampden's out the question he'll not
get to there with ease
To venture walking up that long Hill
means muck up to the knees
And should the rain be fast a falling
he'll be "drookit" to the skin
So Oatlands folk on big match day's
Must Sit and Listen in

Rutherglen he'll never see again
unless he walks for a mile
With the boots were getting now
it's really not worth while
That is why the Folks in Oatlands
when nights are long n bleak
Sitting by their fires and do wonder
if the Wee Red lum's still reek

Let's pray that 1950 a difference
Here will make
That "high Heids" in the council
will give themselves a shake
And in the Corporation we will get
Men with brains
Then Oatlands folk will move around
When they've no fits and pains.

W.S.

The above poem was composed and penned by the late Wullie Scorgie, it was kindly given to me by his son Billy and it was a pleasure for me to retype it out [best as I could]. Wullie was a prolific poem writer and I know that Billy has told me he had composed many many poems in his lifetime but sadly they have been lost over the years.

So thanks to you Billy for forwarding your Da's poem to me and I hope that everyone reading it has enjoyed it as much as me

Bill Mackin.

Also I would like to give thanks to Bill Mackin a fine Glasgow boxing champion from Oatlands, he started off as a light flyweight but won his Scottish title as a bantamweight when he soundly defeated Robert Foy at Meadowbank stadium in 1983. Fair play to you Bill.

The Findlay Family.

Hi Danny I know you're looking for thing's about Oatlands well my grandparents William and Christina Findlay were the first tenants to move in to Oatlands at 12 Granton St they had a son and daughter George and Eileen then William came along to which he was the first baby to be born in Oatlands his Mum and Dad were given a bank for him of Oatlands and the Richmond Park what it was then later on George went to war Eileen got married so that left William later on my grandparents died William got married to Jean so William took over the tenancy of 12 Granton St they had 3 son's Stephen, Leslie, Billy and 3 daughter Alison, Annette, Michelle who all lived happy in a 2 bedroom house my dad William died at 72 years old he stayed in number 12 for all his life my brother Leslie took over the tenancy then so that was 3 generations in one family in one house my brother Leslie still has my dad's bank he was given when he was the first baby born in Oatlands sorry this is so long Danny x

The story above was kindly given to me by Annette Findlay, This is a great piece of Oatlands history Annette and thank you very much for sending it to me. x

This wee story is from Colin Mackie.

Hi Danny....here are some of my shop memories of Oatlands......."My family were good friends with Mr Singh who had the wee grocers shop at the top end of Dalmeny Street (near to Toryglen Street) and my mum used to love it when his wee daughter used to come round to our house her name was Suhki, ...I remember there were times when my mum would send me round (like many families) with a tick note for messages and I would try and add my own written contribution onto it aka sweeties and ginger lol...but Mr Singh wisnae daft and sussed me no bother....Milford Moores shop at the Polmadie Road end of Cramond Street, he used to sell lovely rolls and stewed sausage with onions...Jimmys Cafe, he had a candyfloss machine and an orange juice machine with floating plastic oranges in it, loads of rows of sweety jars, cola cubes, sour plooms, candy balls (filling pullers), strawberry and lemon bon bons....McCowans Dainties, when they were the size of yar haun......or was it just that your hauns were weeir back then lol

Margaret Taylor's Memories...

I liked Mary Hamilton's story of her life in Oatlands. I, too, was born and raised there and we lived at 'this' end of Oatlands, namely 21 Wolseley Street, round the corner from the Ritz cinema. Mary lived at the posh end, with Toryglen Street and Rosebery Street etc. having 'wally closes'.

My husband and I had our first home, a single apartment, in 27 Wolseley Street when we married in 1957. We are soon to celebrate our Golden Wedding Anniversary.

We lived across from the wash house and public baths, and every Friday evening or Saturday morning saw my friends and I queuing up for a bath, rolled up towels under our arms. We sat on wooden benches in our turn, waiting for the raucous voice of the attendant shouting 'Next'.

Woe betide anyone who didn't hear her first time over the roar of the baths filling with water! She would open the door and bawl again, 'Next!' My bath was always much too hot, and I was too scared of her to tell her, and you couldn't cool it as she had a special key for the taps. I would have to wait for ages until it cooled, which had her banging on the door to see if I was alright, or to hurry up, I never knew which. I would finally emerge from the bathroom with my legs red raw, and feeling quite faint.

The wash house served another purpose apart from the doing the weekly wash. The wall in Wolseley Street was always lovely and warm from the boilers, and we stood with our backs and our hands to it on the cold and frosty days We called it "the hot wa", and bounced our balls against it as there was no-one to complain.

We left Oatlands in 1960, and just like Mary, also live in Nitshill, but I will never forget Wolseley Street

Author's note:

Just like so many boys and girls over the years Margaret remembers how we used to all stand with our hands behind our backs leaning on the Hoat wa' to get them warmed up in the Winter time, and it looks like Mary also moved out to Nitshill the same as me and my family did. These memories of the "hoat wa" are forever etched in our memories and I'm so glad that we can share this memory with others of our generation, and future generations to come after us.It all seems so long ago now since this happened and yet it's still fresh in my memory, as I say it is etched in our memories forever.

Story by Danny Gill.

I was born in the Oatlands area of Glasgow and my street Fauldhouse street [where Saint Bonaventures school and the "steamie"=wash-house was situated] was just a five minute walk from the Gorbals. I was born in 1948 and our tenement buildings were the same as the Gorbals, the majority of people were working class and money was tight all round but the community spirit pulled us all together, very few families had tv's or fridges or household appliances that we take for granted nowadays. Yes it was rough and ready [I'm not looking through rose tinted glasses] but my upbringing in those far gone days helped shape me into the person that I became and in my travels as a bricklayer halfway round the world I never ever forgot my backstreet upbringing and the people who might not have much money but were the salt of the earth and although we never had much we all shared.

My tenement building collapsed due to old age in 1961 and my family were moved out to one of the new housing estates being built on the outskirts of Glasgow and I've got to say that I hated living there, I lost all my friends in the south -side of Glasgow and to me life was never the same again, this happened to a lot of families who were "shipped" out in the slum clearance of the '60's and 70's to these new housing estates and life-long friendships were lost but we still have our memories and that can never be taken-away.

Author's note:
The above text was sent by me to Iconic photos e mail address and it was answered by my old pal Billy Graham below.

Hi-Danny,
I was looking for pictures of my old school, Wolseley Street primary when I stumbled on to this site.

I wonder if you remember me, I lived round the corner from you at 51 Wolseley Street, the close between the dairy and the fruit shop. We used to pal around with each other, I have a memory of you and I going to Calderpark Zoo one day but we spent our bus fare home on ice cream and had to walk all the way home to Oatlands. Some going for two kids around 10 years old.

I believe we moved to Nitshill before you did, but I remember meeting you there once. Our mothers must have kept in touch because my mum seem to know how your family were getting on.

I emigrated to Canada in 1981, now living near Toronto. By the way I bought your book Gorbals and Oatlands, hope you're keeping well.

Regards,
Billy Graham

My Reply.

Hello-Billy,
I certainly do remember you, yes you lived up the close between the dairy and Cathys fruit/greengrocers shop. What a great childhood we had Billy, in fact I met Robert Fulton and his brother William at an Oatlands reunion do about a year ago in the Glencairn club (just past Shawfield stadium). Yes Billy our Ma's were good friends and yes I do remember meeting you when we moved to Nitshill. I hope life has been good to you over in Canada, Billy. I mentioned you by name in my latest book "Emah Roo" (Oor Hame) Billy. Isn't this internet a wonderful thing.

I'll speak to you later , take care for now and God Bless all. Your auld pal Danny.

I have a couple of photos of Wolseley st school, the Steamie etc. Perhaps I can send them to you ?

Chaper 13

Poems

Shawfield Stadium.

Fun years ago was watchin Sunday night at the London Paladium.
But Greyhound punter's all headed for a bet at Shawfield Stadium.

Going on Tuesday and Friday night's with money in their Pocket.
Prayin out very loudly their dog wid run like a Supersonic Rocket.

Most punters lost cash as their Greyhound were slow out the stalls.
Diddny have their fare home so was a walk back to the ol Gorbals.

And years ago at Shawfield you hid a fitbaw team called Clyde FC.
But to the supporter's who watched them they were the Bully Wee.

A great wee team they were but now they hiv changed their ground.
Hoping fur better days and praying fame and fortune cood be found.

Beside dugs and fitba you hid speedway racin and a hall fur a dance.
A guy winnin money on Friday nights dug's, = money for romance.

But Greyhound punters are happy people their misery only fleeting.
Cos' if they lost on Tuesday they wur sure to win at the next meeting.

Ma.

A wish of mine for many's a year, as I write my wee poem with pride.
Is to hear once more my Ma's voice in the Tenement's of the soo-side.

Bringing me up like Ma's do lovingly, teaching me right from wrong.
Closing my eyes I can see her washing the stair's, always with a song.

Her words of wisdom installed into all of us wae tender love and care.
And as she aged I loved her more, even as Silver appeared in her hair.

Life for oor Ma's was hard back then, but they'd always see it through.
Making sure ye all had enough to eat, your brothers, sisters and you.

Off to the Steamie wae her weekly washin, Ma done it withoot a moan.
No washin machines in those days, micro wave oven or mobile phone.

We've so much to thank aw our Mothers for more than that I canny say.
'Cos she is the person who made us the men and women we are today.

Your love for me was unconditional but ye passed away when aged 87.
I never got over losing you Ma, as you joined all the Angels in Heaven.

The Shows.

Who remembers year's ago, when we were young and life so serene
And every summer we went to the Shows jist over in Glasgow green.

The Wurlitzer spun roon so fast, and the Ghost train made ye scream.
Weans were eatin toffee apples or candy floss to them it wiz a dream.

Pop music was in the air, as people all gathered there in their throngs.
Some gangs would have a fight, Cumbie, Derry or the Calton Tongs.

Yer Ma and Granny would play housey housey hopin they would win.
Fortune telling by Madame Za Za, but it cost a shillin for you to go in.

Stall owners shouting out come try yer luck and win a coconut or two.
But I never saw anyone win wan they must have been stuck wae glue.

See this is the Shows that I used to know when I wiz a soo side wean.
Dive Bombers and the big Dipper so fast but I'll wont see them again.

'Cause I left old Glesga Toon about a life time ago, as the story goes.
But In my mind I'll always be a soo - side wean going to The Shows.

Primary School.

Remember the days when we aw went to oor Primary school.
We learned our times tables as we used an auld wooden rule.

Makin oor way to school each mornin, trying never to be late.
Because after the Nine O'clock bell the Janny closed the gate.

Ma took ye on your first day, looking on with such great pride.
This happened at our Primary Schools, in all of Glasgow wide.

Sitting in yer seat listening closely to everything you were telt.
'Cos if ye diddny then the Teacher wid give you six of the belt.

We hid plenty of different schools to cover every faith and Ilk.
Sharin wan thing in common, yes that third of a bottle of milk.

Some of us liked learning lessons, I coodny be bothered at aw.
Waiting for the playtime bell, so I could play a game of fitbaw.

Primary school days were great their memory will never cease.
My best memorys, playtime staunin there eatin my Jeely Piece.

Wolseley st school.

Who remembers aw gaun there, we were weans learnin the rule
Boys and lassies attending there, Wolseley st wiz a great school

Bill Hands one of the boys as wiz young James Jamie McKenzie
Colin Mackie oot o music choir, hitting the triangle wae a frenzy.

Myra Hall was wan o the lassies, living opposite that school gate
Left her hoose as the school bell rang, never wance wiz she Late.

Some pupils had their favourites, lovely Miss Christie was a Joy
Takin charge of the music classes, well liked by every girl n boy.

Shelia McCormack Knox passed the 11 plus exam, she was brill
Refusing to go to John St, and went to Calder st up in Govanhill

It was a mixed Playground, boys and lassies mixing quite sweet
But had to enter their own gates, in Logan street n Bilbao street

Happy days for all of us there our school days really wiz a Blast
And have to thank the Teachers there, who taught us in the Past.

Polmadie Rd.

This thoroughfare starts at Rutherglen rd, just aff Richy park.
Where Oatlands folks over the years were so happy as a lark.

Wolseley street and Roseberry street crossin in a straight line.
The Splash and Malls Mire pubs for you and me ,were so fine

Wae Rosebery park Shawfield juniors fitbaw wiz a strict code
Toryglen st where Glen Daly also dwelt off of Polmadie Road

Then you had St Margaret's Church, with stonework very neat
Almost beside it ye had the Pen[d], leading onto Elmfoot street

After passing Kilbride st, stood an industrial estate to the right
And at Polmadie Locomotive Sheds, engine's berthed at night.

While in summer nights of lightness, or winter's nights of dark
Football fans in thousands, marched up to Auld Hampden park

Now Polmadie road is not mentioned much, which is sad to say
But it's still is a vital link in Oatlands as I write my poem today.

The Logan bar

The Logan bar wiz a busy pub, where Oatlands folk did meet
It was on the corner of Rutherglen Rd, n also on Logan street

Opposite was Deefy McGregors shop, with his dug big n lazy
Cos he was deef ye had to shout, and the Alsation went crazy

Just up fae Deefy's you had a bookies, put a bet on every day
Gambling it was illegal then and the Polis took Punter's away

Roon the corner wiz wee Jeannie Frenchies, selling us sweets
And manys a time us Logan st weans went in for penny treats

Canny forget Wolseley st school, where ye never made a fuss
Every day learning your lessons, hopin to pass the eleven plus

Those "new houses" going along Kilbride st were so very neat
Lassies playin peever boys playin fitbaw the length o Logan st

Yet the Logan st that my generation knew, is sadly of the past
Growin up there in Oatlands 50 years ago it really was a blast.

Wee Bonnies.

I went to wee Bonnies primary school jist only one street away
Was taught all of my lesson's by the Teacher's there every day

Some of the teachers spoke so harsh, others had a voice of silk
Who can forget the morning time gettin that wee bottle of milk.

My favourite wiz Mr Jimmy D'Arcy, he was Best of them All
Lessons were soon forgotten as somebody mentioned football.

And playtime wiz magic our runnin around, it would not cease
Well only if for a minute 'till we had eaten our playtime piece."

Lassies aw playing beds/peever, boys all playing wae a fitbaw
And if there wiz a fight then the teacher, wid lay doon the law.

This was wee Bonnies school and us weans were full of zest.
But if we were naughty the teacher's belt gave us six o the best.

Then came the Eleven plus exam, all our cheeks were "aglow".
Top marks meant Holyrood, lesser off to big Bonnies ye'd go.

Oatlands Dream.

Last night I had a dream, as I took a trip down Memory lane
And found myself back in Oatlands where once I wiz a wean.

Oor tenements were still standing, no they hadn't gone at all.
Lassie's were aw playing Peever, Boy's all kickin a football.

At Richmond park feeding the swans, wiz great for you n me.
Then walking along Rutherglen Rd, to spit at the Devils- tree.

In the morning off to school, Wolseley st or Bonnies we'd go.
The future wid change Bonnies name, to that of John Bosco.

Gettin older we would visit pubs, if we were feelin at a loose
Used to do oor back seat winching, in the Ritz Picture Hoose

Those were the days, we were young, and as happy as a Lark.
With yir Da ye'd watch Clyde FC, over by at Shawfield park.

When I woke this mornin my Oatlands dream had took flight.
No need to worry, I'm dreamin about Oatlands again tonight.

Lighting the Fire.

I can remember all of those years ago, and yes God loves a trier.
A ritual duty of my generation, to daily light the Tenement Fire.

But before you could do this,I tell you sincerely ,I am no kiddin.
Ye had to get last night's ashes and dump them all in the midden.

Then you'd hunker doon on your knees yes this was the fire plan
Wae newspaper and kindlin sticks at hand, the firelighting began.

You'd build the sticks like a pyramid so the air cood pass through.
Scattering wee lumps of coal all around it that is what I would do
.
Then lighting the kindling sticks and slowly watch it all smoulder.
Bending doon and blowin air fae yer cheeks tae the fire got bolder.

Then wae yer weans standing watching you, their faces not glum.
A sheet of newspaper oer the openin it wooshed way up the Lum.

That was my generation, now sadly that fire-lighting skill is gone.
Cos today to get some heat in the house, we jist turn the heater on

Rosebery st.

Those lovely Red Sandstone tenements, are now sadly in the past
Where we aw knew everyone, and thote that they wid always last.

And what about all of the shops, going along oor Roseberry street.
Wullie Scorgies newsagents, home made tablet jist coodny be beat

My Pal Jean Shreenan n Tommy Leonard, shared the same landing
Leslies the butcher shop his meat was always of first class standing

See this is where we all grew up, at Dalmeny st we hid Jimmys cafe
Opposite there we had Richy park aff to the swings to have a laugh

Along a bit ye had Billy Moores dairy where we we'd stop to meet
The 101 Trolley Bus it terminated roon the corner in Quensferry st.

Not to forget those "new houses" or as we called them the grey sq
Their lovely wee gardens, and all of the Neighbours gatherin there

This wis the Roseberry st we knew shops gave yer Ma and Da Tick.
Oh to go back and see it again, jist fur a day, oh that wid be magic.

Saturdays.

Saturday's as I recall wiz the best day for us wean's Fixtures
Nae school for us that day, t'was Saturday matinee Pictures.

Life changed I got older, played fur my school team proudly
Played at Glesga green's ash pitches, pals cheered on loudly.

Leavin primary and secondary school, and jobs for us calling.
Satuday's were better, we had a wage, life was so enthralling.

Naebody wanted to work Saturday's, if so then only till noon
Boys wanted to watch the fitba', lassies shopped in the Toon.

Saturday night's you had a few drinks, then onto the dancing.
Nature taking its course boys n girls aw lookin fur romancin.

Suddenly not weans anymore, getting engaged oh ya Dancer.
What better day to get married aye Saturday wiz the Answer.

Reaching my Autumn years I'm an OAP wae bones that creek
I'm Retired noo, havin 1 Sunday, and 6 Saturdays every week.

Lewis's.

Who remembers Lewis's store in Argyle st, so many years ago.
Taken there by your Mother and yer wean's cheek's all a glow.

The size o Lewis's wiz awseome, staff to look after your cares.
Going up and down the escalator, we called them Movin stairs.

Doonstairs wiz their cafeteria for a big plate of Fish and Chip's.
Prices were reasonable and the ice cream made ye lick yer lips.

Best of all wiz the toy dept, it had all oor weans eyes a popping.
Our Ma's never had much money so a lot wiz windae shopping.

When it wiz Christmas time Lewis's windaes wur a sight to see.
Full of fairy light's all flashing, Oh Lewis's was the place to be.

As I grew older and workin, every Friday I had money a plenty.
Visiting their music dept and buying the hits o the Top Twenty.

Lewis's building now has many shops each his their own motto.
Feels like only yesterday us weans queued up for Santas Grotto.

First Day At Work.

Was yer first day at work, a pleasure or Disaster.
Me I started mine wae bricks, concrete n plaster

First day I stood at Saltmarket in the year o1963.
The van picked all the men, but left withoot Me.

My boss diddny tell the driver I'd be at the drop
I phoned, so my 1st day was at the Joiners Shop

That's how my 1st day went no covered in glory
I'm sure you reading my poem has his/her story

Wiz your 1st day at work good, or a big let-doon
Did ye work in a factory, or a shop o'er the Toon

Did ye get sent for "Tartan paint" to yer Dismay.
Or a "Long Staun" and you'd stand there all day

Oh my first day at work I do remember very well
And jist like you my friend ye have a story to tell.

The Auld Tin Bath.

Who remembers getting washed in the sink, or the old tin bath
At the time I felt like greetin but as I look back noo I can laugh

I wid dread Sunday nights and the sound of that whistlin kettle
Because wae it's boiling watter Ma wid fill up that bath a metal

The auldest wean went in first, like thay were King o the Castle
Us younger weans had to wait oor turn, hating all of this Hassle

Well your Ma scrubbed you that hard, that yer skin wid turn rid
People o my generation know this is the truth, I really don't kid

Drying yourself in front of the open fire, feeling good and sleek
Listenin to your siblings saying, Ma I had a bath only last week

But as you grew older, your life changed to being a bit dreamy
Cos yer Ma gave you money for a hoat bath in the old Steamie

Now I have a bathroom so enormous, it would give ye a Fright
But I'll never forget that auld tin bath, and every Sunday Night.

Washin the Stairs.

This weekly chore in the tenements wiz done wae loving care.
When your Ma or the Neighbour, took turns to wash the stair.

Now oor Ma's had it aw timed to Perfection, to do their chore.
The weans at school Postman had been, into the stair she tore.

The stairs first of all got a sweep so no dust was a laying there.
Then wae a pail of hot soapy watter, your Ma washed the stair.

On hands and knees your Mammy knelt, working like a Navvy.
Makin the stairs spotless, especially round the stairheid Lavvy.

Each side o the stair got pipe chalked, to a dead brilliant white.
When they were finished, our tenement stairs looked a delight.

But if yer Ma was taken ill and her outlook didn't look dreamy.
She still took her turn, or she would be the talk of the Steamie.

This was the tenement I grew up in, closin my eyes they thrive.
Wish to God I was back there cause my Ma would still be alive.

The Sensational 70's----- Part 1.

So many things happened this decade at home and abroad too
Decimilisation, Punk Music, and Flares to mention only a few

Gorbals clearance, tenements gone, multi storys up to the sky
Oor Tartan clad Bay City Roller sang by by baby, baby by by

13 people shot dead in Derry, we prayed for peace Tomorrow
The Ibrox disaster 66 dead, old firm fans united in true sorrow

Snooker gave to us Alex Higgins he was a genius with his cue
Abba won the Eurovision song contest wae smash hit Waterloo

Heath took us intae the Common Market, no Vote did Ted seek
He tried to face the miners doon, aw we got was the 3 day week

Richard Nixon ended the Vietnam war, with peace and Honour
His Presidency ended over Watergate n soon he was a "Gonner"

Tv gave us the Sweeney wae Dennis Waterman and John Thaw
Cinema gave us the Godfather, best Gangster film of them Aw.

The Sensational 70's ----Part 2.

Who can forget that '76 long hot summer sun shining every day
David Bowie as Ziggy Stardust, Rod Stewart sang Maggie May

Tv's Coronation st had Hilda Ogden and Mavis Reilly was dotty
Captain Kirk in the Starship Enterprise said beam me up Scotty

Cassius Clay= noo Muhammed Ali wiz boxing champ Supreme
Ally McLeod off to Argentina, wae the world cup Scottish team

Sadly Elvis Presley died, as the whole music world was in shock
T'was like only yesterday, we heard him singing Jailhouse Rock

Bruce Forsythe's catchphrease, "nice to see you, to see you nice"
Red Rum won the Grand National, not once nor twice but thrice

Britain had its first woman Prime Minister, no one to match her
No pal to the working classes was that Tyrant Maggie Thatcher

Roger Moore wiz the new James Bond, gadgets given by old Q.
Noo the 70's ended what would the 80's bring to me and to you.

The Swinging 60's--- Part 1.

They say if ye remember the 60's, then you weren't really there
Well I can remember every year of it wae great music in the air

The Gorbals clearance had started, oor Tenement's bit the Dust
Dr No with Sean Connery at the cinema, to see 007 wiz a must

Hippy colonies in San Francisco aw into drugs of every manner
TV gave us Doctor Who, Coronation St gave to us Elsie Tanner

President Kennedy assassinated a part of me also died that day
America was still bombing Vietnam wae its new President LBJ

Mary Quant and the Mini-skirt, fashions crazy in Carnaby street
Sandie Shaw won the Eurovision song contest, in her Bare Feet.

Scotland--3 England--2 at Wembley, Jim Baxter stole the Show
Celtic and Rangers both in European Finals, "Go Glasgow Go"

Jist a few events in the swinging 60's which ended far too soon
The highlight being of course, when Man walked on the Moon.

The Swinging 60's ----Part 2.

Elvis came oot the US Army, aw the lassies dreams came True.
The Beatles burst on the Pop scene wae a hit song Love Me Do

The Maginificent 7 wiz a cowboy film, Gunfighters so Resilient.
Good guys won, baddies lost, Yul Brynner and co were brilliant

In 62/3 we had an Arctic winter, sub-zero temperatures freezing
The Profumo affair wae Christine Keeler scandalously "teasing"

Free love and the Permissive Society, all helped on by "The Pill"
Boxing gave us Cassius Clay, watchin him box was such a thrill

"Dr Zhivago" in the Cinema, with Julie Christie and Omar Sharif
The Aberfan disaster, children dead and all of their Family Grief

Procol Harlum gave us a haunting song -A Whiter Shade Of Pale
The great train robbery so audacious, Ronnie Bigg's escaping jail

So much happened in the "Swingin 60's", events never Forgotten
The Sinful 70's the next decade, Punk music with Johhny Rotten.

Epilogue

Well folks, that is my story of Oatlands over and I hope you have enjoyed coming on a walk with me through all the streets to a time when the old tenements were still standing and the open coal fires were still being used. It's actually been a labour of love for me although it was hard to try and remember all the shops names and peoples names too, remember we are going back to the 1950's and I had to do a lot of head scratching while also relying on other people's memories too and I sincerely thank everyone who took the time to help me.

My memories as I keep saying is of Oatlands in that era of the tenements and "the new houses" built between the war years, it was sad when some of the tenements started to be demolished in the 1970's of course bearing in my mind that because of the position of the British oxygen company's depot up near Polmadie railway sheds the regeneration plan was "put on ice" because of the health hazard [explosion/fire]. In 1977 one of the propane gas tanks caught fire, sending flames a hundred feet up in the air and 160 firemen fought the blaze.

Of course there was a refurbishment carried out on the red sandstone tenements in the mid 70's but it was a "botched up job". People said that they would have preferred to have lived in the old places as the soundproofing was bad and windows were bad fitting , dry rot, rising damp etc, and building materials were left out in the open to all the elements. There were "plots" erected in the new Oatlands leisure centre at Polmadie rd/Elmfoot st but I think that people knew that no matter what there was going to be a complete regeneration of Oatlands it was just a matter of time.

What I tried to do in my book was rekindle the memories of the "auld days" when people seemed to have more time for each other as opposed to today and we had that unbreakable community spirit, then with demolition of the old buildings that were our homes we were scattered all over the place, some moving to other parts of Glasgow

[mainly the housing schemes] or even going to other countries. Personally I think that Glasgow city planners did a very good job with layout of the new houses and gardens for peoples with bathrooms and inside toilets too but it will never replace in my mind that era of the auld tenements when we would all stop in the streets and have a natter while going for the messages and life was so less stressful as it is today but as the old saying goes life must go on.

We have all said it before "wouldn't it be great to go back in time even for a day to that time of the auld days", perhaps one day that will happen but in the meantime I hope that when anybody reads my book then they will transported back in time, and no matter wherever we are in the world that era of Oatlands where we all grew up will always stay alive.

I was very proud to be able to write this book and I'm glad that I could mention a few people by name, the shops we used, pubs we had a drink in and that feeling of this was where we belonged. So wherever you are in this old world of ours I hope you enjoyed the memories of "Once upon a time in Glasgow's Oatlands" because this is how it used to be.

God Bless all.

The End

Street Index

Close numbers + names

Alice street.

Isabel Horan, close number 3.

Brian Donnelly, Eamon Monaghen, close number 15.

Bilbao street.

With the exception of the janitors house in Wolseley st school, there were no houses here, Bilbao st was a mini-industrial estate.

Braehead street.

Arthur McGuire, close number 61.

Brian Morris, close number 69.

Gallaghers, Dorrens, Lynahs, close number [?] unknown.

Glen Daly, Louis Robison, the Ross family, Slowey family, close number [?] unknown.

Cramond street.

Daniel Crossan, Davy Leishman, close number 11.

Angela Gillies, John and Annie McKinnon, Rose McQueen, Vinnie and Kay O'Boy, all at close number 14.

May Sweeney Bishop, close number 15.

Mick Flavin, close number 23.

White family, Daly's, McFadden family, Nina [?], McGarvie family, Margaret + John Gemmell, all lived at close number 26.

Donny Turner, close number 27.

May Miller, close number 56.

Danny McGhee, James+Anna Kerr, close number 62.

Lisa Gillen, close number 72.

Colin Mackie, Meg Sey, Miller family, Alex Graham + family, Martin + Betty Curran's family, Josie Bagbsy, all at close number 74.

Dalmeny street.

Joe Wilson, close number 4.

Angela Roberts, the Wilson family, close number 22.

Janice Flanagan, McWhitters, Montagues, Hanlon family, Mrs Cassidy, all at close number 29.

Frances Welsh, close number 35.

McHugh family, Mr Singh, Christina Milarvie Quarrell, close number 60.

Jacqueline Brown + family, Turnbulls, Bislands, Mr McDevitt, Hydmans, Johnstons, all at close number 61.

Elmfoot street.

Frank McLintock, close number 7. - Agnes + Frances Connolly, close no.16.

Mrs McMahon, close number 26.

Frances McKinnon, close number 27.

Sadie Quigley, close number [?] new houses.

George O'Donnell, Honeymans, the Duffs, Cameron family, the Semples, Devany family all at close number 49.

Elaine McNulty, close number 76.

Fauldhouse street.

Mrs Elizabeth Newall, close number 16.

Lawrence family, the Healeys, Clark family, Chas Lee, Mr Thom senior, The Gill family, Mr + Mrs Thom, Jenny Tarbet, Wullie Glasgow, Andrew Ewing, all at close number 40.

Tam Gillon, Mrs Quinn, Phil Gillon, Mr Douglas, the Hendry family, The Bouchers, Potts family, Mrs Wilson, all at close number 32.

Billy Morton, Ian Davidson, close number [?].

Mr Reid, close number [?] - Mrs Henderson, close number [?].

Granton street.

Margaret Bonar McCulloch, O'Lones, Gough's, McLaffertys,, O'Donnell's, Duncans, the Howitt family, all lived at close number 1.

Gilmours, Dyers, Lamonts, Mrs Crosbie, close number 2.

The McKelvie family, close number 3.

Rab Hay and Family, the Ham family, Lisa Gillen, Marie Reilly, Betty Park and the Nivens all at close number 4.

Mrs McGill, Jackie Green, Sally Feeley, Yvonne Morgan, the McQuarrie family, Pattons all at close number 5.

Colin Mackie, Derek McKenzie, Mrs Sharkey + family, Karen Hamilton, Lisa Gillen, all at close number 7.

Frances McBride, [Lynch], Taylors, McClung's, Watt family, Littlers, Millers, McFayden, Burns, Hunters all at close number 11.

Michelle Findlay, close number 12. - Neil+Daniel Crossan, close number 14.

Kilbride street.

Oats family, Anderson family. Close number [?] unknown.

Logan street.

Shelia McCormack Knox, Pall family, Mellors, Wisons, McQuarries, Smilie, another Pall family, all at close number 2.

Shelia McCormack Knox, Kemps, Grahams, Stoddart family, Tomineys, Thompsons, all at close number 10.

Jim Clark, Honeymans, Andsersons, Tominey family. Close number 16.

Mary Higgins , close number 27.

Linda Stephenson, close number 29.

Myra Hall [Rowling], Lettie and Jeff Torrington, Mr Judge, Rowling family.

Mrs McLure, Mrs McNeil, Docherty family all lived at close number 35.

Cathie Murray, close number 41.

The Kean family, Debra McCann, Annie Docherty, close number 101.

Polmadie road.

Billy Scorgie, the Tartaglia family, Theodore Scorgie, Lizzie Smith, Jim + Phyliss Hunter, Johnnie + Betty Walker, Mrs Robb, Peter+Susan Muir, Barnie Keenan and family, all at close number 3.

May Miller, close number 21.

Angela Gillies, Boyle family, Breigh O'Donnell Salina, all close number 45.

Bonner family, James family, Kings, Mrs Young, Mr Kay, Mr + Mrs Stuart, Mr McLeod, Mr Rigby, Mrs Shepard, all at close number 51.

The Sweeney family, close number 94 - Paul Heggarty close number 102.

Anne McNulty, close number [?] unknown.

Queensferry street.

Lynda McGovern, close number [?] unknown.

Rosebery street.

Heather Hope Wilkinson, close number 16.

Lynda McGovern, [Lowe family] close number 19.

Linda May Moore Ross, close number 45.

Alexis Rutherford, close number 48.

Maria O'Neill, close number 51.

Angela Shreenan [Burns], Jean Shreenan, Tommy Leonard+Ma, all at close number 52.

Mackie family, Maureen Dougan, Ann-marie McKelvie, Maureen Hendry, Robert Corlett, all at close number 63.

Lorraine Park, McCuskers, Blakes, at close number 103.

Mackies, Mr +Mrs Smith, the Campbell family, Mr Waugh, Mr McGarvie, McDaid's, all at close number 123.

Rab Hay, close number 129.

Diane Ferry, James, Jamie McKenzie, close number 135.

Leanne Gardner, close number 148.

David Hodge+family, Bill and Theresa Stephenson, close number 153.

Derek Ian Elder, close number 159.

Angela Roberts, Angela Shreenan, Janet McKenzie, close number 173.

John Noble, Davy Holt. close numbers [?] unknown.

Rosyth street.

The Howitt family, close number 1.

Nellie + Donald Steel, Annie Hay, Mrs Nimmo, Joe Kelly, close number 2.

Grace Brown, close number 4.

Anne Marie McKee, Anne Marie McDonald, Mulholland family, Blount family, Cuthbertsons, O'Donnells, Hutchison family, all at close number 7.

Evelyn McQuarrie, Adams family, Hughes family, Hall's, Dorrans, Levys, and Donachie family, all at close number 9.

Linda Quinn, Linda Keane, McVeys, Sutherland family, Fowlers, Black family and Whyte family, Gary Taylor, close number 11.

Rutherglen road.

Betty Miller, close number [?] unknown between Fauldhouse st /Braehead st.

Mr Guthrie, close number 614.

Brian Donnelly close number 664.

Mrs McCulloch, close number 696.

Mitchell Crombie, Mrs Boyle, close number [?] uknown it was the last close at junction of Rutherglen rd /Fauldhouse st.

Tommy and Liz Gilmour, close number [?] unknown close next to the Logan bar at junction of Rutherglen rd/Logan st.

Gibbs family, close [?] unknown.

Mike Hoggs family, Shillinglaws, Frances Shaw, O'Mara family, Garretts, Stewart family, Hughie Hendry's family, close numbers [?] unknown.

Toryglen street.

Glen, Ella Daly, Linda Moore, Mrs Eccles, close number 3. - Park's close 21.

Lisa Gillen, Margaret Ballingall, the Sweeney family, Glasgow's, Alexandra family, Stirlings, Mullhollands, Miller family, all at close number 33.

Bill Hands, Alexanders, Charlie George, close number 81.

Wolseley st.

Billy Harvie, The Daly family, close number 12.

George Mullen , Margaret Taylor, close number 21.

Mrs Docherty and son John, the Taylors, close number 27.

Fulton family, Andrew West, close number 40.

My Granny + Granda Hendry, Mick McLeavey, Marion and Malky Davidson, the Brown family, Connie Beattie, Workmans, close number 48.

Billy Graham, Baltoushla family, Workmans family, all at close number 51.

McFaddens, close number [?] unknown, - Jean Friel, close number unknown.

Jeanette Russell, Clancy family, close number 63.

Mrs Innes and son Peter, close number [?] unknown.

Rosemary McKee Robertson, close number 129.

Tricia Anderson, Patricia Rankin, the McAlpines, Mitchells, Carrol/Curr, McLean, Hobbins, Mullen family, all at close number 176.

Haig family, Martin Curran, McFaydens, Roberts family, Docherty family, all at close number 179.

George Motherwell+family, close number 180.

Mrs Cavanagh, Motherwells, close number 184.

Mrs Boyle, Mrs Downie, close number 188.

Bill Mackin, Karen Doherty + family, close number 196.

Alice McLaughlin, Turner family, close number 210.

Printed in Great Britain
by Amazon